CW00820332

WITH FLYING COLOURS

WITH FLYING COLOURS

THE PIRELLI ALBUM OF MOTOR SPORT

BY LJK SETRIGHT, DEREK FORSYTH AND ROBERT NEWMAN

Stanley Paul
London Melbourne Auckland Johannesburg

Stanley Paul & Co. Ltd

An imprint of Century Hutchinson Ltd
Brookmount House, 62-65 Chandos Place,
Covent Garden, London WC2N 4NW

Century Hutchinson Australia (Pty) Ltd
PO Box 496, 16-22 Church Street, Hawthorn,
Melbourne, Victoria 3122

Century Hutchinson New Zealand Limited
32-34 View Road, PO Box 40-086,
Glenfield, Auckland 10

Century Hutchinson South Africa (Pty) Ltd
PO Box 337, Bergvlei 2012, South Africa

First published 1987

Set in Univers Medium Condensed Italic

Printed in Spain by Printer industria gráfica s.a.,
Barcelona

ISBN 0 09 171180 0

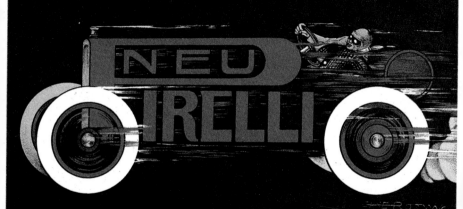

A CELEBRATION OF PIRELLI'S 80TH YEAR IN MOTOR SPORT 1907-1987

CONTENTS

WITH FLYING COLOURS

WITH FLYING COLOURS
THE PIRELLI ALBUM OF MOTOR SPORT

An orderly succession of prominent aces, a regular procession of dominant nations, and always with the same notion – that there is something ennobling, instructive, intoxicating, in driving a good car on a challenging road, faster than anyone else. In the disorderly processions of eminent races much older than the car, men would habitually and compulsively seek the same elevation, and hope to demonstrate the same superiority, in urging that fleet and gullible creature the horse to competitive effort. Is racing therefore always a contest between men?

There was a steward at the 1962 Brussels Grand Prix who stated quite categorically that it was a race for machines, not for men. There were drivers who, in the late 1970s, complained quite vociferously that the differences between one GP car and another at that time were such as to make the differences between one driver and another insignificant. Yet, if the race be between machines, who but men will take credit for those which are victorious? Pride of ownership, pride of creation, pride in association, these are the things that impel men to blazon their cars' names on their clothes and on their trophies.

Does that make motoring competition commercial? It always was, but seldom has it been only commercial: at various times it has been in the grip of nationalism, patriotism, communism, eclecticism, vandalism and once or twice of mysticism. We have seen a race rigged at Tripoli by drivers who had banded together to profit from an associated state lottery; we have seen a race wrecked at Indianapolis by dishonest abuse of the cautionary light-signals.

Corruption is not a modern disease. At the very first Grand Prix race, in 1906, the cars had to be guarded overnight (it was a two-day race) by the three noble stewards who were the only members of the organising body who were free from commercial interests and could therefore be trusted. Sabotage was a constant worry in those distant days, when the surreptitious notching of an external copper oil-pipe could ensure fatigue failure in a race that lasted for several vibratory hours. Yet we called the activity a sport then, as we call it a sport now; and a sport it has always been, no less than athletics or cricket, horse-racing or boar-hunting. The driver who deliberately baulks his challenger today is applauded, where a quarter of a century ago he would have been severely reprimanded, and half a century ago it would never have occurred to him to do it; but in the 1930s races were won by minutes, in the 1950s by seconds, and today by mere fractions – if not by infractions.

The dead heat nevertheless remains an oddity, reserved for triumphant team-members who have managed to get together to swamp the finishing-line after a long sports-car race at Le Mans or Daytona. Yet there was a spate of such things in 1961, when the Dutch, French and Solitude Grands Prix all ended with a show of that bitter strife bred by almost precisely equal combinations of car and driver. As Francis Bacon observed rather earlier, 'there is little friendship in the world, and least of all between equals.'

There have been stranger finishes than those. There was the winning spinning driver who crossed the line backwards and was sent back down the road to do it again properly. There was another who took the chequered flag while upside-down – a position which later made rally-driver Carlsson legendary, so often did he adopt it while setting his little Saab to ski the snows of the Scandinavian rallies. Scarcely had he become famous than all rally drivers began to make a fetish of driving sideways, something that racing drivers had stopped doing years earlier.

The skills and judgment developed by the greatest drivers are marvellous to ponder but not always wondrous to behold. The smooth precise man who never wastes an inch nor ever makes an error is assumed by the crowd to have a better car; they take more pleasure in the man who teeters on a perpetual seesaw of slide and counterslide. So it is that popular appreciation of drivers is sometimes coloured by their entertainment value. The modern man submerged in scientific marvels which allow him no scope for fancy wheelplay makes his appeal to the grandstands and the cameras by a display of aggression; he makes the same impression as the mighty man of valour at the beginning of the century, practically standing up to the steering wheel the better to wrestle with it. In the intervening decades, armplay

was what folk loved to see.

They loved Nuvolari, dancing in his cockpit; and Moss, tweaking his wheel all the way; and Rosemeyer, scything through corners that others only took in snippets. But they never took much notice of slender Cagno, deft and delicate in his handling of Fiat and Itala giants in the days of racing's genesis; or of restrained Caracciola, secure on rainswept roads while slower men went sliding into the scenery. They paid scant attention to meticulous Prost, until he suddenly stood before them as a champion. They could not help but admire Jim Clark, visibly faster than all about him, but only the tyre technicians knew how incredibly balanced was his use of all four corners of the car, to a degree not even approached by any of his contemporaries.

Clark was possibly the finest of them all, but it is impossible to be certain. Fangio must surely appear in any shortlist of three, Caracciola in any of two; but who is to make the final stroke of the pen, and later wonder about Brooks or Bordino, Varzi or Wimille, Lauda or Ascari? Three

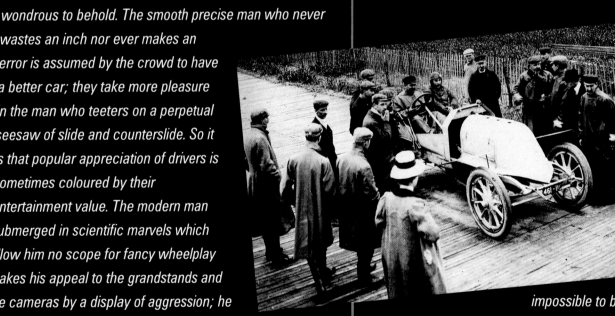

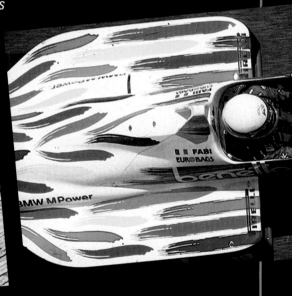

WITH FLYING COLOURS

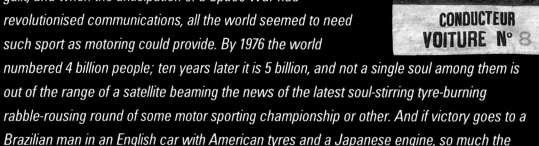

of those six have been praised as outstanding by the very men we have appraised as the greatest; and who should know better than another driver? And what does he know, if he be a racing man, of the virtuosity of the rally men – of Makinen and Mikkola, especially? And how does one rate the special gifts of those whose reckonings are in the splinters of seconds whittled from a Worcestershire hill or chipped from some Alpine cleavage by the likes of Mays or Stuck? Or how class those whose care of car, and stomach for speed, must be cultivated all through the nightlong daylong devilry and drudgery of Le Mans or Spa, those whose names are as long honoured as Barnato, Gendebien, Bell, Ickx?

Men and women galore and multicoloured make the mosaic that pictures motoring as a sport. They do not have to win championships to be memorable: Crook and Gerard, Sommer and Rosier, Junek and Ivanowski, scores and hundreds of names are notable, thousands necessary for the Byzantine patterning of events crowding the calendar ever thicker each year.

From France and America they spread first to Germany and England, to Italy and Austria, to Russia and Spain and all of Europe. When the Great War had redrawn the boundaries of nations and extended the domain of the internal combustion engine (staff cars were raced across Egypt then, and record-breakers across Australia), all the world came to know the sport which motoring was. When the World War had redistributed the wealth of the nations, when the Vietnam War had redistributed much of the guilt, and when the anticipation of a Space War had revolutionised communications, all the world seemed to need such sport as motoring could provide. By 1976 the world numbered 4 billion people; ten years later it is 5 billion, and not a single soul among them is out of the range of a satellite beaming the news of the latest soul-stirring tyre-burning rabble-rousing round of some motor sporting championship or other. And if victory goes to a Brazilian man in an English car with American tyres and a Japanese engine, so much the better.

We have had enough of nationalism in our sport. Doubtless it served its purposes at the times, reviving the morale of the downcast, raising the standards of the repressed, and occasionally spitting in the eye of the overweening. France was unquestionably the leader until Italy in 1907, and Germany soon after, stepped in to challenge her. It looked like being France again after the Great War, but in 1922 Mussolini came to power in Italy and adopted as a major part of his foreign policy the reduction of French influence. Was it coincidence that from 1922 Italy dominated motor racing until Hitler had settled into power a dozen years later, when his brand of National Socialism used motor racing as an advertising medium to impress the world?

Nothing like that ever happened again. Perhaps the sport of motoring was never so sporting as in the two decades after the fall of Hitler. It was sheer human spirit that made Italy top dog for the first of those decades, and dogged enthusiasm that made Britain supreme for the second. Then it was the turn of the French, with a new generation of keenly schooled drivers enough to supply all

WITH FLYING COLOURS

the leading teams until the present era when everything from the oil companies to the television subtitles is truly international.

The USA could so easily have swamped the lot. Only sympathy for the splendour and simplicity of American isolation can explain why it did not; but the Land of the Free is well enough represented, in the list of the truly great and influential carmakers of racing history, by the most freethinking (and one of the most splendidly simple) of them all, the Chaparral. Goodness knows there have been cars by the hundreds to cement that mosaic of drivers by the thousands; but the names that have significantly altered the course of motor-racing history and had a lasting influence on its engineering have been few indeed. Peugeot, Fiat, Mercedes-Benz, Cooper, Lotus and Chaparral are those names, in chronological order; and if others favoured by enthusiasts or deified by idolators be examined, they will be seen only as arch exponents of established principles, or entrenched defenders of established interests. The name of Porsche might grudgingly be added in recognition of the special case for the sports car; and the competition development of the touring car to flower as the rallying

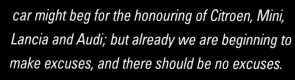

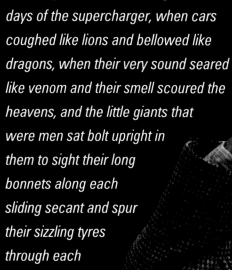

car might beg for the honouring of Citroen, Mini, Lancia and Audi; but already we are beginning to make excuses, and there should be no excuses.

None of them needs any excuses. They were all marvellous, all beautiful, the successful and the failures alike. There is a beautiful integrity in the uncompromising and dauntingly competent stance of today's cars, wide and low and sticky with rubber, clean and complex as a surgical theatre, a blare in the ears and a blur in the eyes and a fireproofed gauntlet flung in the face of relevance. So was there a beautiful intensity in the tiny cigar-bodied cars of the early 1960s, their waxing tyres strangely remote on fragile suspensions summoning an image of water boatmen, those slender insects which go skimming the surface with oars that seem barely to touch the water's meniscus. Their tiny jewelled engines sang a pure high strain, a clear clarion with six scales and a tiny polished wood-tipped gear-switch to pluck each in turn from the ecstatic coils of exhaust pipes.

What cataracts came spouting from the trumpets of the generation earlier! What variety there was, as V8 vied with straight eight, fat four with slim six, and as much argument raged about the right shape for a chassis or the right lines for a body as about the architecture of an engine. Most noble rage of all, though, was surely the fury of the last days of the supercharger, when cars coughed like lions and bellowed like dragons, when their very sound seared like venom and their smell scoured the heavens, and the little giants that were men sat bolt upright in them to sight their long bonnets along each sliding secant and spur their sizzling tyres through each

drifting tangent. How the photographers loved to catch them head-on in their four-wheel drifts, how the public thrilled to watch them in profile on their full-swill razzle, glorious in detonating defeat and uproarious in explosive victory!

But then to go back to the vintage years and to look and listen with senses not yet sated – were not these machines beautiful, in their proportions as in their promise? When superchargers were new and springs were stiff, when engines twisted in the torture of their own heat and drivers blistered in their wake, when the very pores of the cars opened with the anguished hours to lard the lean earth with their oily sweat, was it not bliss to be a spectator? And very heaven to be a competitor, making music with a forged gearlever that begged to be used, while making peace with a fractious clutch that begged to be left alone? Making constant corrections, even along the straights, with a steering wheel that kicked you for your pains – and making whoopee afterwards with

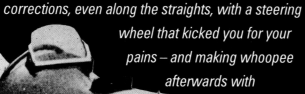

fashionable friends who loved you for your valour? That was when a car's proportions were like those of man, with the equilibrium of the Golden Mean and the consonance of the harmonic triangle, when a car's dimensions were based on a human scale and its pretensions were an extension of human values.

Beyond them, before them, loomed the giants. They were not as heavy as they looked – nothing short of a railway locomotive could be as heavy as some of them looked – nor as clumsy; but because they were so large, and because their engines turned so slowly, they were often faster than they looked, and much faster than they sounded. Like all the giants of history, they were soon cut down; but while they held sway, they were magnificent. Sculptors were inspired by them, painters bemused by them. The Manifesto of Modern Art (it was a great time for manifesti, on

behalf of every cult from Dada to Communism) proclaimed as its new ideal of naked beauty the racing car, with its huge red bonnet from which came winding and fat a polished copper exhaust breathing fire and shrapnel… Without a doubt, the modern artists of the old days knew what was beautiful.

So do we today. So did every motoring enthusiast, always. Men and machinery and motion make a picture as surely as they make music, and the notion of sport invests even the bleakest picture with a beauty like no other. It is that beauty which this Pirelli book sets out to capture. The mosaic is too vast and too detailed for its every tesselation to be attested; but as in every case where art transcends science, or where genes imprint Jones, each part stands as conceptual surety for the whole.

A portrait of Nuvolari is a snapshot of an era; a picture of a Jaguar echoes every one that

has howled through the French night; a cloud of dust and a glint of light, and all rallying is remembered.

The part played by Pirelli in all this is not explicit in this celebration of a century of the sport. Not a picture has been chosen with them in mind, nor is it part of the author's brief to blow their trumpet. All that needs to be explained is that Pirelli have been involved for eighty years, starting with the winner of the Peking-Paris race in 1907; and if you wonder what is special about eighty years, there is a Psalm which declares it a sign of special

strength. That strength must have helped their first Targa Florio win in 1913, not to mention the Buenos Aires-Cordoba event in the following year. But this is to be no chronicle of victories; there have been too many. It is no critique of designs; they have been too various. Suffice it that Georges Boillot won his second Grand Prix on them, Tony Brooks his first, Fangio his last, Berger their most recent. Bentley won their first team prize on them, rally champions and endurance racers have saved their necks and reputations on them; and there are still surprises, and maybe prizes, in store.

Never mind the future: that is another motoring century, full of bridges not yet to be crossed. The past is gone, but not yet to be lost: not its men nor its machines, not its shapes nor its colours. The future may never present another past like it; let us save it, and savour it.

GROWING UP AMONG GIANTS

It was a confused infancy that motor sport enjoyed. The enjoyment lay in the fact that the motor industry was more confused still – and even that was nothing compared with the utter confusion, the head-rattling alternation between daze and dazzle, suffered by the people at large. Yet, out of all the rattles and the ever louder bangs – and, sadly, a scream or two – there emerged a pattern, settled in this century's first decade and spreading over most of this world's leading industrial nations.

The great annual Grands Prix became the major events; but hillclimbs were not to be decried, the beginnings of rallying were not to be denied, and record-breaking amazed the public when the world's fastest cars outsped aeroplanes.

Then, in the last years before the Great War, the giants were overthrown. Engines became smaller, worked harder, and invited a new romance between engineers and motorists. Racing-car design underwent a revolution – because it was a time for revolutions.

1894 - 1917

*Left, top: De Dion
tractor in the Paris-Rouen event of 1894*

*Left, bottom: 1894:
a Peugeot in the Paris-Rouen event*

Right: 1895 Paris-Bordeaux: Levassor

Left: 1898 Paris-Amsterdam-Paris: the start

Above: A Bollée in the Tour de France, 1899

Right: Hammering around France:
a Panhard in the 1899 Tour

Dust, tallow, and kettledrums: that was motor racing then, in the faltering cockcrow of a petrol-scented century. Crude and comical they were, and tentative and terrifying by turns, the cars which bellowed bluff and chirruped of friction as they took their stand to defy time and all comers. What had come from all time was a new age, just a hundred years ago, an age so youthful in idealism and manful in ambition that it could not wait longer for steam to replace the horse, could wait no longer on the promise of wings to cheat the wheel. Markus and Daimler, Butler and Benz, stubborn thinkers and passionate mechanics had created motor vehicles, had internalised combustion and commotion; they had pitted them against the road, and in their naïve defiance the cars had come out conquerors. Now it was time to pit them against each other.

The first organized attempt at a motoring competition was a flop, as first things often are. Perhaps 1897 was a bit too premature for a French journal to promote such a thing; at any rate only one entrant turned up for the start. For a few more years, motoring competition would be informal: whether encounters on the road were arranged or accidental, it would be the spur of the moment, the spur of pride or curiosity, of an aggressive temperament or of a sporting wager, that would bring them together. Amidst every uncertainty from the thermodynamic to the hermetic, the only probability was that the road on which they met would be French.

Deep-bosomed France, the very mother of Chauvinism, did a remarkably hospitable job of wet-nursing the motor car and the aeroplane, and turned a tolerantly dim eye to the unfortunate fact that the former came from Germany and the latter from America. Britain was locked in the happy embrace of steam, legacy of her industrial revolution; Italy and Germany, each only recently unified politically by industrious revolution, were neither of them yet unified socially; looming Russia had yet to revolt. Only France and America, having built themselves revolutionary new societies at a time when Gibbon had only just finished chronicling

Centre: Emil Jellinek,
father of Maja and Mercédès

Right: Camille Jenatzy

*Marcel Renault, the
man who beat the Arlberg Express*

*Below: La Jamais
Contente, the electric streamliner
which first exceeded a mile a minute*

*Centre, top: Marcel Renault
en route from Paris to victory at Vienna*

*Centre, bottom: Louis Renault at the
weighing-in before the Paris-Vienna race*

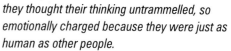

Hub-cap from Porter's Paris-Madrid
Wolseley, which hit a wall
and killed his mechanic Nixon

French ballet: Paris-Madrid

Strip, left to right:

Gabriel (Mors) at fantastic speed,
in frightening crowds,
during the fatal Paris-Madrid race

Louis Renault leaving Paris 1903. Down
that road to Madrid, his brother was killed

Drive through the
dust and steer by the treetops: Paris-Madrid

the decline and fall of ancient Rome, were mentally and materially equipped to foster anything as iconoclastic as the motor car – so rationally aimed, because they thought their thinking untrammelled, so emotionally charged because they were just as human as other people.

If America became the car's breeding-ground, France was donor of the genes. By 1891 the basic imprint which would shape the car for generations to come had been established by Panhard, and in the decade before the USA could start to build the future, France made history. In 1894 it proved feasible to stage a reliability trial over the 79 miles from Paris to Rouen. Fastest of the 21 competitors was an articulated De Dion, but the steam tractor which hauled a disappointingly horsey carriage needed two crewmen, which was not at all in the spirit of independence that the organizers sought to encourage. They gave the top prizes to Peugeot and Panhard instead, and set about planning a real race for the following year.

It was a greater event by a whole order of magnitude, casting out from Paris to Bordeaux and reeling in again to cover 732 miles. To quieten protests about the perils of speed, the major award was reserved for four-seaters, which were obviously practical vehicles; but two-seaters, though they were deemed deliberate devotion to speed at all costs, were nevertheless admitted. Recorded as fastest four-seater was a Peugeot which finished third, in a matter of 60 hours – but what everybody remembered was the winner, a two-seater Panhard averaging 15mph to complete the round trip in just over two wearying days and wicklit nights. Historians still argue whether the driver, Levassor, supped on soup or champagne at his hasty Bordeaux turnabout; none will concede that he might have taken both, though none could deny that he must have needed both. So much for historians…

As for history, it now came thick and fast. The

Right: 1903 Mercédès, Paris-Madrid.
It was not always safe to steer by the treetops

Below, right:
Cooling the tyres of Baron de Caters' Mercédès

Fitters' final preparations in a French farmyard

city-to-city race was a perfect demonstration of the motor car's potential for door-to-door diminution of life's losses of time and chance. The burgeoning French motor industry saw every justification for creating purpose-built racing cars, for inviting the public to enjoy the spectacle, for whipping up every enthusiasm that might be turned to custom. While America mustered two starters and one finisher (the little Duryea, still in the prototype stage after two years as the nation's first horseless buggy) in a frostbitten race from Chicago to Evanston, France looked on 1895 as an entree to a perpetual feast of speed.

Time and chance worked their ways upon that menu, as each demonstration was diminished in perfection by losses of life. The years 1896 to 1903 saw a succession of scandalously dangerous road races, usually from Paris to another city, each more ambitious, more ruthlessly realistic, more callously indifferent to consequences than the last. France was not big enough for the visionaries of that age: after racing to Marseilles, they raced to Amsterdam, to Berlin, to Vienna, and finally (though they did not know with what deathly finality) they set out for Madrid.

These were great races, the hazards horrific, the drivers heroic, the cars gigantic. Thundering like duns at a poet's door, skipping like the stones they flung across the rutted roads, these spider-wheeled chariots were usually big, often heavy, invariably ill-balanced and frequently ill-mannered, intractable inchoate triumphs of audacity over perspicacity. Men were still learning how to make cars go well, having barely discovered how to make them go at all; but men were learning very fast – perhaps because of the spur of competition – and by the beginning of the twentieth century standards had risen considerably. No more was brutish size enough.

It was a lightweight car which taught the most salutary lesson. Fastest of all in the 1902 Paris-Vienna race was the Renault running in the minor category: it only had about 40 bhp, but for all its comfortable size it weighed only 1200 lbs, whereas the big cars weighed a ton and could not match its

Rented farmyards and inns were
the usual resort of racers in preparation

Previous page:

Inset, left: Wagner's Darracq in the last
Gordon Bennett race

Main picture:
Thèry, nicknamed "Le Chronomètre",
winning the Gordon Bennett cup in 1905

Strip, top to bottom:

Thèry's Richard-
Brasier, fastest of all Gordon Bennett racers

1905 Gordon Bennett :
Wolseley, low-slung but under-powered

British Racing Green is actually
Parsons' Napier Green – the shade worn
by this car in the 1905 Gordon Bennett race

Right: Heath brings his Panhard through Neufchateau in the 1904 Circuit des Ardennes

Below, right: Most successful with Panhard, Heath was an American living in France

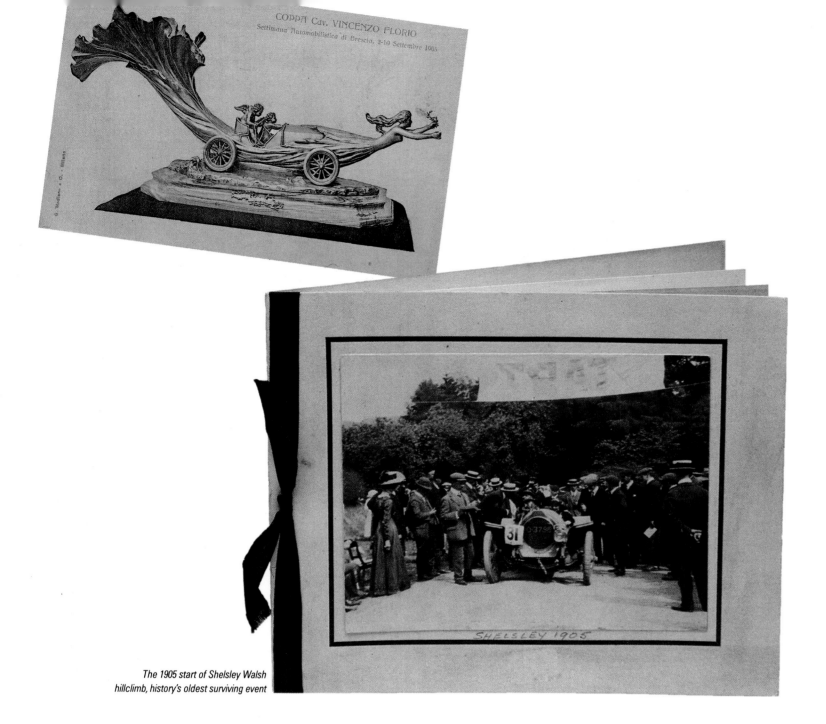

COPPA Cav. VINCENZO FLORIO
Settimana Automobilistica di Brescia, 2-10 Settembre 1905

SHELSLEY 1905

The 1905 start of Shelsley Walsh
hillclimb, history's oldest surviving event

agility. Marcel Renault, brother of constructor Louis, reached the finish at Vienna so fast that he had to wait for the officials to turn up and meet him there. What an object lesson! In Britain one could average 50 mph on the London-Cheltenham train, or see 90 behind Gooch's North Star, yet 20 mph in a car was deemed an offence against the human body, against God, and against organised society – in ascending order of seriousness. German attitudes were not much healthier, although races had been held from Berlin to Leipzig, and Frankfurt to Koln; but here was this commerce-hungry Frenchman making light of a 5000 ft Alpine pass to reach Vienna seven hours faster than the Arlberg Express!

To such extent as the resentment was commercial, it worked both ways; for there were Germans in the sport too. One of them in particular used to do well in the events of the Nice Speed Week (a race from Marseilles, a sprint along the Promenade des Anglais, and a climb up the hill to La Turbie) where the cream of society flocked each sun-seeking winter. The diplomatic Emil Jellinek moved in these high circles, and drove heavy Daimlers at high speeds with good results, so that he became exceedingly influential in the sale of cars to the polite and prosperous. The only handicap he encountered was the Teutonic name of Daimler, distasteful to the French; so he insisted that Germany's new Daimler model for 1901 be named after his younger daughter.

The son of an Hungarian rabbi, Jellinek led an adventurous early life in South America, where he swept up a beautiful Spanish bride – and that is how the car came to be called Mercédès. Old Gottlieb Daimler was already dead, and his brilliant technician Maybach was more concerned to realise some of his engineering ambitions, so the 1901 Mercédès was enormously influential. The most authoritative design of the half-century, it was soon to sire some very effective racing cars; but racing was soon to be effectively very different.

It was The Race of Death which did it, the infamous ill-fated Paris-Madrid disaster of 1903. Strongly supported by 179 entrants, and publicized

Main picture: Wagner's Darracq
rounds the pole-squatters
in Long Island for the 1906 Vanderbilt Cup

Inset: Vincenzo Lancia (driving
for Fiat), second in the 1906 Vanderbilt Cup

Below, top: 1906:
Mrs Vanderbilt and Mrs Smith turn heads

Below, bottom: Long Island, 1906:
Wagner's winning Darracq

up to the hilt, it drew 100,000 Parisians to see the cars start (one by one, against the clock) from Versailles, and they thronged the roads all the way to the end of the first stage at Bordeaux. They thronged unchecked, undisciplined, untutored in the dangers they approached, unable to conceive the speeds that the cars would reach. They filled the narrow round-crowned roads, parting only reluctantly at the last moment to let a speeding car pass; but they were not always quick enough. Stray children, stray dogs, oxen, the clouds of dust raised by the cars, all added to the drivers' confusion; competitors and spectators alike were killed, their mangled remains sometimes discovered only after the blinding dust-clouds had settled. Gabriel, the fastest man to get through to Bordeaux, admitted that he sometimes had to steer his huge Mors by the poplar-tops that alone were visible to show the way the road went.

The race was stopped. All motor racing might have been stopped; but the sport had already been diversifying, and it was the newer kinds of competitions which saved it. The sprints and hillclimbs at Nice were examples of events growing in popularity: the first European hillclimb, a club outing in 1899, was a full-blooded speed event by 1902. The Alps were there for storming, and in Britain there were hillside bridle paths which offered a shorter but subtler challenge: one such, begun at Shelsley Walsh in 1905, retains the longest continuous history of all sporting events. Americans from 1916 would rise to the 14,000 ft challenge of Pike's Peak, approached by 12½ miles of dirt road winding into the clouds.

Climbing crude paths was a test of reliability in the early days; speed itself hardly mattered. Britain's Thousand Miles Trial of 1900 was meant to prove the practicality of the touring car, as was the original Tour de France; by 1905 the car's practicality could be taken for granted, and trials became speed-oriented handicaps for 'touring' cars. The Herkomer and Prinz Heinrich events, staged in the Austrian Alps first with the participation and secondly with the patronage of

Weybridge Motor Track. "The Finishing Straight."

Far left, centre:
The association of Brooklands
with horsepower goes back a long way

Far left, bottom:
They built Brooklands fast,
but printed picture postcards even faster

Centre, top:
The last patch: a pose to celebrate
completion of track repairs at Brooklands

Centre, bottom: Bridge over the river
Wey, built in Hennebique's Patent
Ferro-Concrete on Ferro-Concrete Piles

Below: Mr Timekeeper
King-Farlow's Brooklands clocks

Right, main picture:
Opposite lock, 1906-style, by Louis Wagner

Inset, top: Coated long and light
for the 1906 TT, the well-known
(not a bad driver, but a great
publicist) Australian associated
mostly with Napier and AC, S. F. Edge

Inset bottom: Rolls Racing:
the "Light 20" on its winning way in the 1906 TT

Right: Petralia Sottana,
on the 1907 Targa Florio route

Opposite: Brescia, 1907:
Coppa della Velocità – and how!

Left to right:

*Standers and
movers at the very first Grand Prix*

Cagno's Itala at the start of the 1906 GP

*Noted for deftness, delicacy, precision
and exceptional speed, Alessandro Cagno
was distinguished among giants*

CIRCUIT DE LA SEINE INFERIEURE · 1907

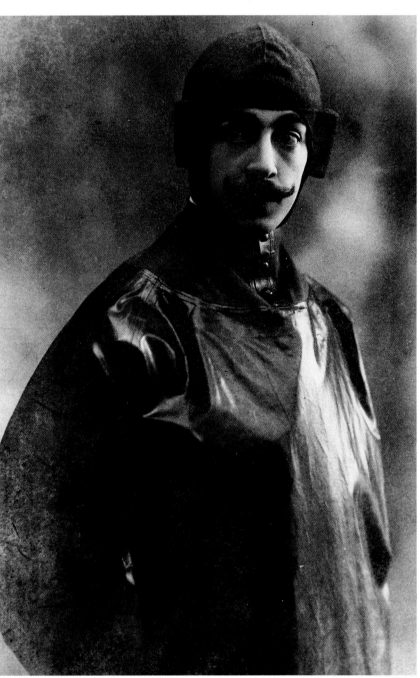

His Royal Highness, shared with the Isle of Man Tourist Trophy the early development of the sports car; combined with contemporary efforts to organize a winter convergence upon Monte Carlo, they also nurtured what would become rallying.

It was all very deliberate, very earnest, very well intentioned; but what the people wanted was, like Gibbon's ancient Romans, circuses. There was no substitute for the real pure racing car, for sheer undiluted speed. If the world's fastest cars could no longer be raced from city to city, let them be raced in some sort of closed circuit where the public could be better controlled; perhaps the cars would then prove even faster.

There had been since 1900 some ill-supported races for the cup put up by James Gordon Bennett, the sporting and prodigiously wealthy scion of the New York Herald. He had introduced the idea of national teams, each country fielding three cars made entirely within its boundaries and painted in national colours. Whatever country won the first race would play host to the second, and so on – until in 1902 England won, and that created a problem. The common-law freedom of the King's highways could not be suspended for any motor race; so the event was packed off to Ireland, where a course could be found by looping a few roads together. The 1903 Gordon Bennett event, in the same season as the last of the open-road epics, was the first closed-circuit motor race.

It was also the first to reveal that the passions aroused in motor racing were not entirely sporting. The German team cars were sabotaged shortly before the event, and were hastily replaced by stripped touring Mercédès – one of which won.

The French were disgusted with the whole thing. They were allowed only three entries, like any other nation, when they had enough different makes to swamp the rest of the world. As soon as they had control of the race (that is, when they had won it twice again, in 1904 and 1905) they suppressed it, and put in its stead the race which was destined to grow from an annual event in France to a fortnightly circus taking in a third of the world: the Grand Prix.

Above: …stood at the door of the morning… The winning Pekin-Paris Itala on display outside the offices of the newspaper "Le Matin", which sponsored the race

Main picture: Over the Joinville bridge, another 8 miles to go and 16,000 behind. The drive from Pekin took 16 tyres and 60 days

Opposite: Prince Borghese congratulates Pirelli on his arrival from Pekin

Below: "Also ran" – and stumbled, and was pushed and pulled and hoisted – and finished!

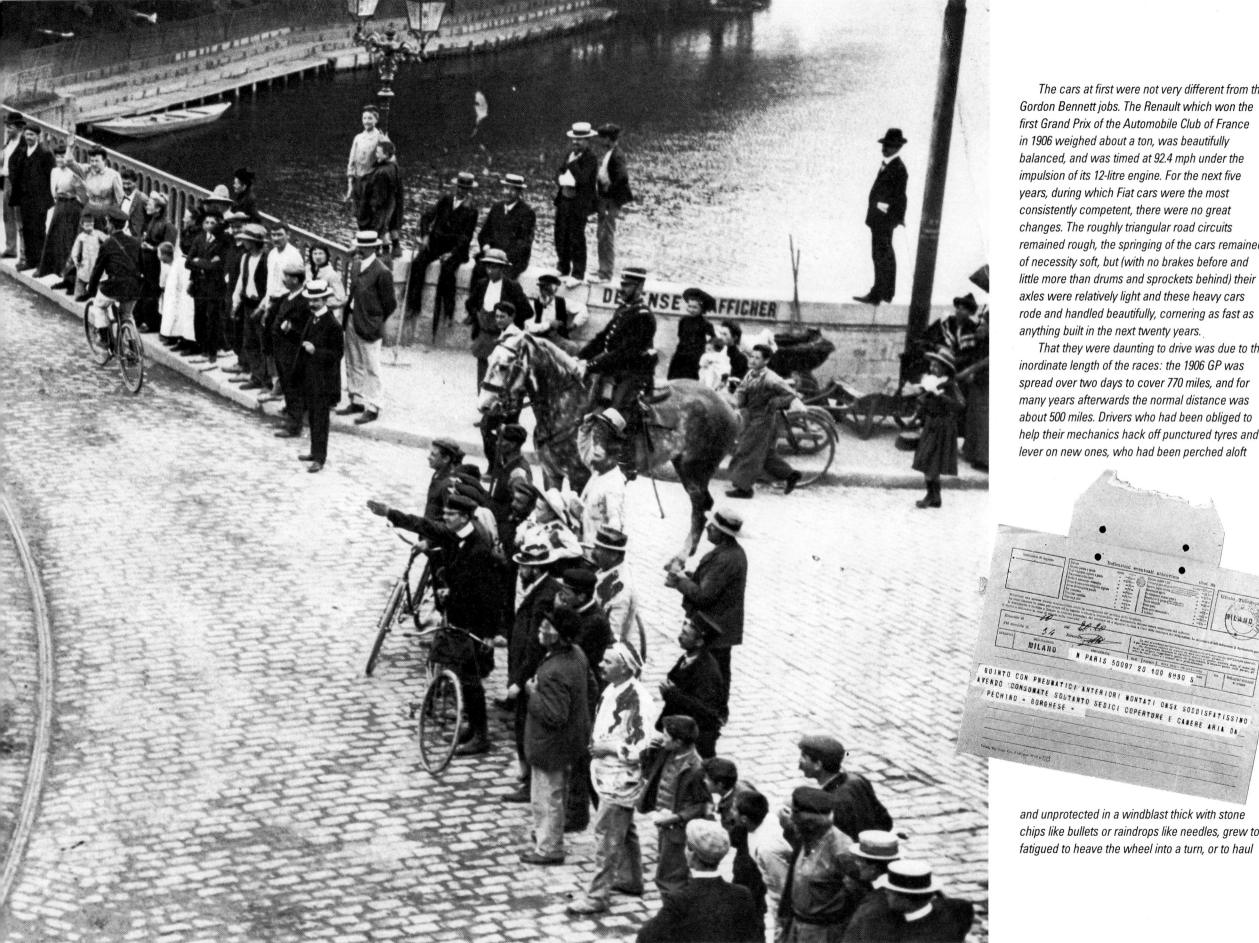

The cars at first were not very different from the Gordon Bennett jobs. The Renault which won the first Grand Prix of the Automobile Club of France in 1906 weighed about a ton, was beautifully balanced, and was timed at 92.4 mph under the impulsion of its 12-litre engine. For the next five years, during which Fiat cars were the most consistently competent, there were no great changes. The roughly triangular road circuits remained rough, the springing of the cars remained of necessity soft, but (with no brakes before and little more than drums and sprockets behind) their axles were relatively light and these heavy cars rode and handled beautifully, cornering as fast as anything built in the next twenty years.

That they were daunting to drive was due to the inordinate length of the races: the 1906 GP was spread over two days to cover 770 miles, and for many years afterwards the normal distance was about 500 miles. Drivers who had been obliged to help their mechanics hack off punctured tyres and lever on new ones, who had been perched aloft

and unprotected in a windblast thick with stone chips like bullets or raindrops like needles, grew too fatigued to heave the wheel into a turn, or to haul

An Itala fit for a prince – and still fit after carrying him from Pekin to victory in Paris

PÉKIN–PARIS_1907　　　　EN SIBÉRIE

Le Prince Scipion Borgaese Gagnant du Raid "PÉKIN-PARIS"
Sur sa Voiture "ITALA" 24 HP.

(Voyage accompli en 44 jours de marche effective)

Émile Sevelinge 07

Top to bottom:

Race tyre depot, 1907

Cerda, 1907:
the grandstand flanked the road into town –

– the main road

*Centre: Circuit des Ardennes,
1907: Wilhelm on a Métallurgique*

Right, top to bottom:

*Buffet luncheon during
the 1907 French Grand Prix*

*Footbridges kept the people in circulation
when an early GP ran through the town*

Felice Nazzaro in 1907

*Below: 1907 lightweight:
Menard's Delage at Rambouillet*

*Opposite:
Lancia's Fiat at pre-race fuelling in 1907*

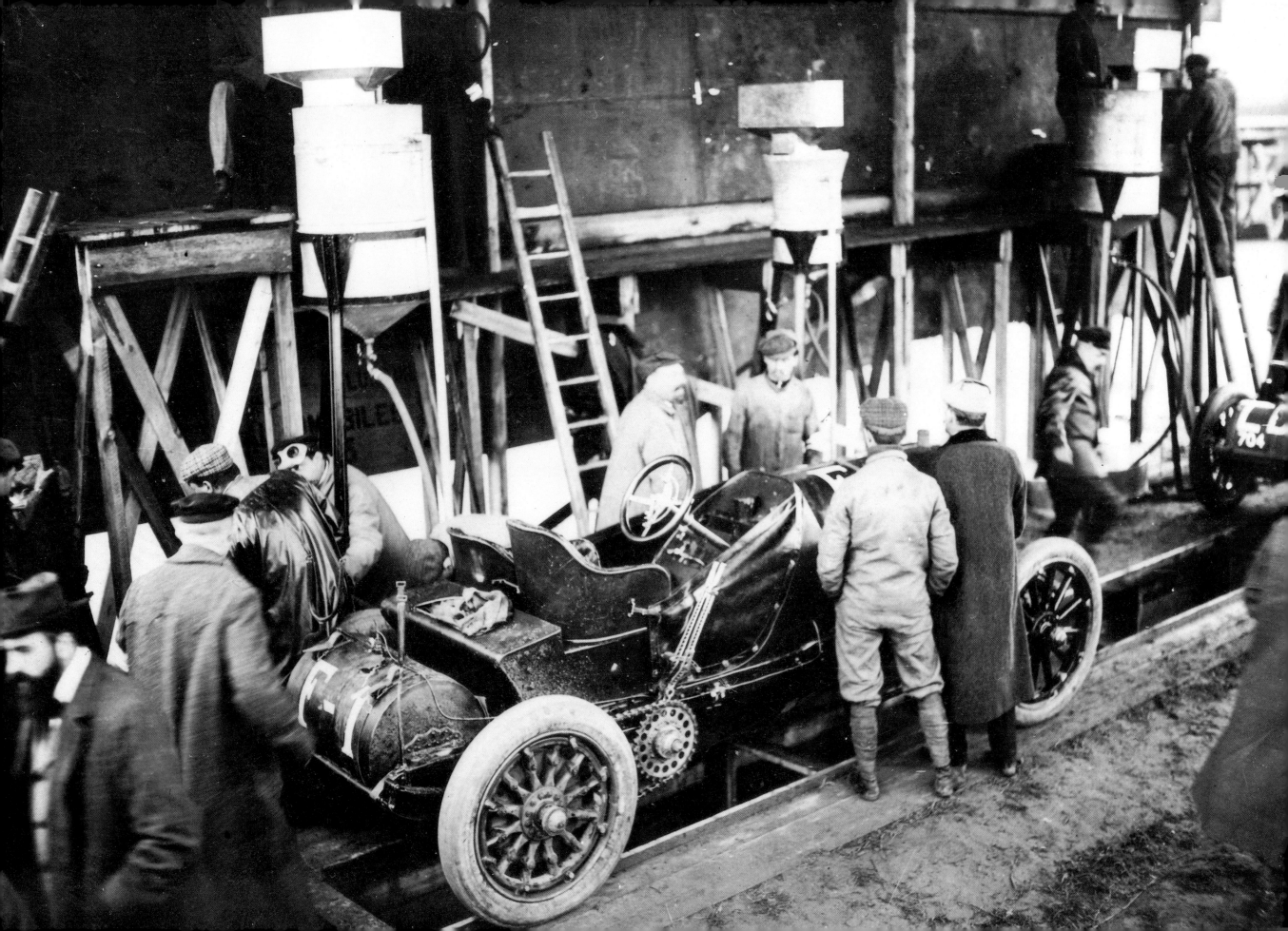

CIRCUITO DI
BOLOGNA
1908

*Demountable wheelrims speeded
tyre changes from 1906 onwards. Minoia gives
his De Dietrich the service in 1908 at Bologna*

*Above: Match race
at Brooklands, 1908: Fiat v Napier*

Centre, top to bottom:

*Hémèry (Benz), winner of the 1908
race from St Petersburg to Moscow*

*A funeral on the Moscow road,
ahead of the cars racing from St Petersburg*

*St Petersburg-Moscow:
the 1908 race route under 'Cossack' guard*

*Right, top: Early European closed-
circuit races were on triangular courses
outside a town, with a forked junction
in the town providing the sharpest corner*

*Right, bottom: Independent front
suspension in 1908: Sizaire-Naudin
in the Coupe des Voiturettes at Palermo*

Circuit de la Seine-Inferieure

Right: Beautifully prepared Benz team ready for the 1908 GP

Far right: Targa Florio photographers were fond of this corner, on the climb into the Sicilian hills. Here Trucca drives an Isotta Fraschini in 1908

Kaiser's Cup Race
Daimler

*An English Daimler
in pursuit of the Kaiserpreis*

Prinz Heinrich Fahrt
und andere Sportszenen
1909

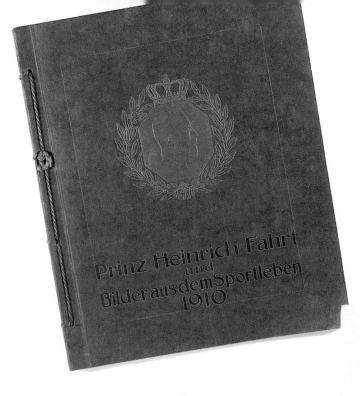

The Start   Kaiser's Cup

Only one man in the factory
was strong enough to start this Daimler

on the brakes as hard as they must. And, truth to tell, after a few hours the spectators were not exactly excited any longer.

Few of them were drivers, after all. Few of those sweaty pedestrians, their suits stiff and shiny with ingrained dirt, their skirts as grimy as the brooms they emulated, their smell rivalling the hot oil wafted in the wake of each passing car, could appreciate the skills of cornering, the perils of braking. Only in the waistcoat pockets of the well-heeled would there be a watch to monitor the relative positions of drivers who had started at 90-second intervals. What the people wanted to see, once the novelty of actually seeing cars had worn off, was real fast intelligible massed-start races. A proper racing track should provide it.

Brooklands, first and most famous, was built in Britain where racing on the roads was prohibited. A masterpiece of high-speed earthmoving and concreting, it was readied by massed muscles in 1907. Men and horses made it, horsey men governed it; the very fastest cars could sustain top speed all around its bankings, the very dullest spectators could understand it. The Europeans, who considered that cars were meant to be driven on real roads at whatever speeds those roads might allow, despised it; the Americans, across whose vast land the intricacies of road-racing seemed irrelevant, took a hint from it and built a more compact Indianapolis. By 1911 they too had settled on 500 miles as a proper length for what has survived as the oldest original race.

Until 1970, the Targa Florio held that honour. Inaugurated fifty days before the first Grand Prix, it traced a long and harrowing course, on roads rougher than in any other major race, in the mountains and along the coastline of Sicily. Conceived by a devoted motorist, Vincenzo Florio, it encouraged cars that were agile but not unstable, cars with the best possible steering and roadholding and braking, with adequate strength and ample stamina. It discouraged cars that were grossly heavy or grievously underpowered; and although it was one of the slowest, it was also one of the most difficult and one of the greatest, of the

Above: Gorgeous Georges

Centre: André Boillot was not so dwarfed by his Peugeot at Boulogne, but did not mind autographing this sketch

Right, top: Pirelli's first GP victory: Boillot (Peugeot) in 1913

Right, bottom: Opposite lock, 1913-style: Georges Boillot winning on the Côte du Ventoux (on Pirellis, on a Peugeot, for that matter) in 1913

Below: When Nazzaro sent his congratulations to Pirelli, he had just lowered the Targa Florio record by four hours!

John Bryan
Boulogne

Right: Porporato drives to a Gregoire victory in the Coupe de la Sarthe, 1913

Far right: Rigal's Peugeot in the 1913 Coupe de l'Auto at Boulogne

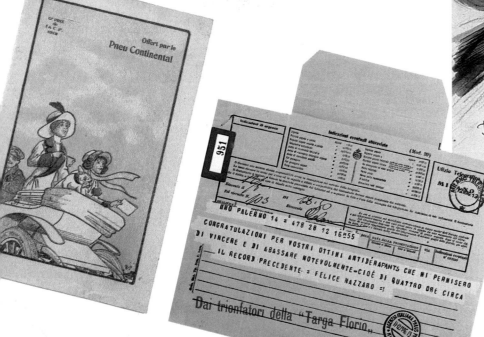

1913: starters for the French cyclecar GP

great road races of which it was eventually the last.

For a long time the Targa Florio attracted Grand Prix racers, but already in 1911 they were beginning to change. The potential superiority of a lighter leaner tauter car was shown in 1912 when a 7.6-litre Peugeot won (with more than a little luck) from a slightly faster and very much bigger Fiat. The trend was confirmed in 1913 when Peugeot won again; and by 1914 the rules had brought the maximum size of the GP engine down to a mere 4½ litres. Once again Peugeot was prominent, once again in the wildly adulated hands of Georges Boillot. Now that cars were smaller they had to work harder, and the drivers had to be more deft: surely none was more so than Boillot then, making the most of his new four-wheel brakes to keep his car on the limit until, on the very last lap of the circuit at Lyon, it was quite worn out. Spirit and patriotism could do no more; not only was Peugeot defeated, but also France. A sullen silent crowd watched stolid Christian Lautenschlager lead the fast, finely trained and faultlessly disciplined Mercédès team to a 1-2-3 victory.

59

One of those Mercédès was then shipped to the USA, where in 1915 Ralph DePalma (an Italian-born American) beat a Peugeot driven by Dario Resta (an Italian-born naturalised Englishman) to win the Indianapolis 500 Miles race. Resta won in 1916, when DePalma's entry was refused (he had been trying to negotiate a high fee for his appearance); but the battle between France and Germany had by then been 21 months of such thunder as no car ever uttered. In that year, fighter pilot Georges Boillot was killed in the air over Germany; there was very little dust, and the drums were muffled.

Left: Now do you see why they were called "the pits"?

Right: Cutting it fine in 1913: proof of the precision of the Pirelli-shod Peugeot

Wet weather goggles, 1911

Previous page, left: Lyon 1914:
Lautenschlager's winning Mercédès

Previous page, right:
1914 pit-stop for Wagner's Mercédès

Right: Days of tow
and grease and fibrous smocks:
Christian Lautenschlager cleans his hands

Dashing Georges Boillot,
trying so hard to win the 1914 GP for France

VINTAGE YEARS

    Now every nation had its hero, for the festering post-war discontent fostered nationalism that in turn fostered the sport; and it was still truly a sport, in which the amateur spirit could and did thrive.

    Racing itself began to thrive, in this speculative forcing-house. The Grands Prix proliferated; elegantly engineered cars, created specifically for them, set new standards of technical brilliance and tantalising behaviour, standards not slow to set a faster pace for sports cars. Long-distance races for sports or touring cars were thus born to a distinguished future, while the Monte Carlo Rally began to take shape. Hillclimbers reached a peak of frenzy; in furious single-mindedness, the track racers of America were as frenetic as any.

    There were accidents, of course; but the biggest crash was on Wall Street…

1918 - 1933

Board track racing, USA

Centre, top: Spare wheel upright
in the tail, a 1921 fashion set by this Ballot
in the French GP

Centre, bottom: Hammer and tongs, Ballot and
Duesenberg, in the 1921 GP de l'ACF. The road was
to get worse later

Below: Just look at those
stones! And this was
the 1921 French GP circuit, for road-racing!

Captain Archie Frazer-Nash
*after winning his class in a 1921 race in
the GN. Its V-twin engine used
only 6 gallons of fuel in covering 200 miles at
over 71 mph, but also 2½ gallons of castor oil!*

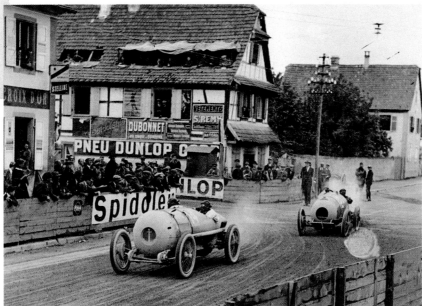

Top: Fiat set new fashions, 1922

Centre: 1922 notions
of aerodynamics, by Ballot and Bugatti

Bottom: Fiat pit-stop, 1922 GP de l'ACF

The war to end all wars, they called it – those who survived. They proclaimed a new world, a world fit for heroes to live in; and a new world it certainly seemed, for the war had been socially the most revolutionary of all time. For heroes, though, there was no immediate demand – not even in motor racing.

Outside the USA and Sicily, there was no motor racing of any consequence until 1921; the British and French had conspired to prevent it, seeing that neither wished to be bothered just then. For the single-minded masters of the Targa Florio, it was no bother at all; as for the Americans, falling happily back into rich isolation, they were beyond the reach of conspiracy. An old Peugeot won the Indianapolis 500 in 1919, but it was an American car which won in 1920, the new Frontenac – even if it was a Frenchman, Gaston Chevrolet, who drove it. His Swiss elder brother was the great Louis Chevrolet, who built the car; and it won again in 1921 with a real American at the wheel, one-eyed Tommy Milton.

It was an old Peugeot which won the 1919 Targa Florio, too, spinning tail-first over the finishing line and ordered back to do it again properly. That victory was emotional as well as theatrical: the driver was André, younger brother of the late Georges Boillot.

No more looking back, after that: 1921 was the year when new cars came to sweep away the metal relics and mental debris of a bygone age. The war had taught us technology – we learn fast when our lives depend on it – and now there was new stuff for making cars, new ways of keeping them oiled, new ways to make them go and even better new ways to make them stop.

Most noticeable of all was not that the cars looked smaller, but that they sounded so different. The gaping bull of Bashan boom of the Edwardian giant echoed only off the Brooklands bankings; the new cars rippled out a solid eight-cylinder roar, their lovingly crafted cranks spinning at unprecedented rates. Exquisitely built, the new cars were; the deeper you burrowed, the more beauty you found, and the multiplicity of identical parts

Top, left: A Bentley in the 1922 TT

Top, right: Running
his Sunbeam wide in the wet: Segrave
at Governor's Bridge in the IoM TT, 1922

Bottom, left: Starting grid for
the 1922 TT, Bentleys in line ahead
on the left. In their first appearance,
they won the team prize – on Pirellis

Bottom, right:
The 1922 Trophy did not go to a Tourist,
but the 3-litre Bentley which
came second was truly a stripped tourer

The 1922 TT Bentley
does not yet have the familiar radiator

Above: Nicola Romeo,
flanked by Rimini and Ferrari at Monza in 1923

Centre:
A Fiat 501 breaks the record
from Singapore to Kuala Lumpur in 1923

Overleaf:

Left: A concrete imitation of
a road-racing circuit was
eventually laid inside the track at Brooklands

Right: Bumpy bankings fostered
chassis built for strength rather than agility

PROGRAMME
SAT. SEPT. 20TH   PRICE ONE SHILLING

200 MILES RACE
FOR LIGHT CARS UNDER 1500 c.c. AT BROOKLANDS.

ORGANISED BY THE JUNIOR CAR CLUB

Opposite:

*Top: The road was
mere dirt for the 1923 French GP*

*Bottom: JG Parry-Thomas in "Babs",
the Land Speed Record contender
which eventually killed him*

Left, top to bottom:

*Bruno Mussolini, fighter-pilot
son of the Duce, was a keen driver*

*Antonio Ascari, in the car, is about to die.
His son, Alberto, will one day be killed at the
wheel too*

*André Dubonnet,
famous for diverse things, was also a
fine driver. He shook the racers with
this tulipwood-bodied Hispano-Suiza*

Centre, top to bottom:

*Major Harvey, designer of the Alvis
tries his handiwork at Shelsley Walsh*

*Little Alberto Ascari,
escorted at his father's funeral
by devoted mechanic Ramponi*

*Bugatti's tiny "tank" streamliners
before the 1923 GP at Tours*

which made up the fashionable new straight eights created a repetitious beauty of its own, intricately patterned as an English cathedral screen or the skin of those no less beautiful and clean-lined lizards under the Sicilian sun.

It was a Californian sun which shone on Harry Armenius Miller, whose clairvoyant ideas were translated by a soft-spoken draughtsman with beautiful hands. Leo Goossen's designs defined the classical American racing engine for forty years to come, but it was as Millers that they were first famed, in simply beautiful chassis that streaked round the banked board tracks flung up by speculators wherever Indianapolis seemed too distant. As the board tracks made way for building lots, or were fired for the insurance money, the dirt tracks came into their peculiarly American own; but there was always Indy, and before long the Millers were supreme there, showing the world the way to go with front-wheel drive and gung-ho drivers.

A Duesenberg came from the USA in 1921 to show Europe how to do it, in the first post-war Grand Prix. It went away with a narrow victory, and acquired a Miller engine before it won at Indy the following year. Europe let it go without any reluctance; an even better engine was almost ready to take the stage.

Beautiful and clean-lined as never before, the new Fiats were the first racers to have wind-tunnel proof of drag and lift abatement. More significantly, they made the running with brilliant new engines which, when their superchargers set a new fashion, became models for nearly every notable GP car of the next forty years. Fiat, who had been the most consistently formidable contestants of prewar years, would not stay long in racing, though their brilliant team of designers was to be head-hunted without remorse by rivals. Theirs were not the cars to beat, but the cars to copy – preferably with an ex-Fiat designer to impose authority upon imitation. Sunbeam did it first; Alfa Romeo did it best, and reigned supreme until the era ended in 1934.

No, not quite supreme. In Alsace there was an instinctive idiosyncratic Italian who did things in his

Alfa Romeo P2 team, 1925

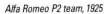

Alfa Romeo P2 team, 1925

Above: Helmet, brassard, ex Antonio Ascari

Overleaf: Dario Resta (Sunbeam) in vain pursuit of Louis Wagner (Alfa Romeo) during the 1924 French GP. This corner of Lyon was a junction known as Les Sept Chemins, and is still recognisable today; but the Alfa Romeo is a museum piece, Wagner died in 1960, and Resta in 1924

OGDEN'S CIGARETTES

SHELSLEY WALSH HILL CLIMB, JULY 11

OGDEN'S CIGARETTES

CIRCUIT DE DIEPPE (1,500 C.C. CLASS), JULY 26

OGDEN'S CIGARETTES

CIRCUIT DE DIEPPE (OVER 1,500 C.C. CLASS), JULY 26

OGDEN'S CIGARETTES

SAND RACE, SKEGNESS; CARR WINNING THE FINAL, JULY 18

OGDEN'S CIGARETTES

GERMAN GRAND PRIX (1,500 C.C. CLASS), JULY 19

OGDEN'S CIGARETTES

R.A.C. INTERNATIONAL TOURIST TROPHY, ULSTER, AUGUST 22

OGDEN'S CIGARETTES

RELAY RACE, BROOKLANDS, JULY 25

OGDEN'S CIGARETTES

MONT VENTOUX HILL CLIMB, AUG. 30

OGDEN'S CIGARETTES

BELGIAN 24-HOURS RACE, JULY 4-5

OGDEN'S CIGARETTES

IRISH GRAND PRIX, SAORSTAT CUP, JULY 5

Lightweights at the start of a Brooklands 200-miler

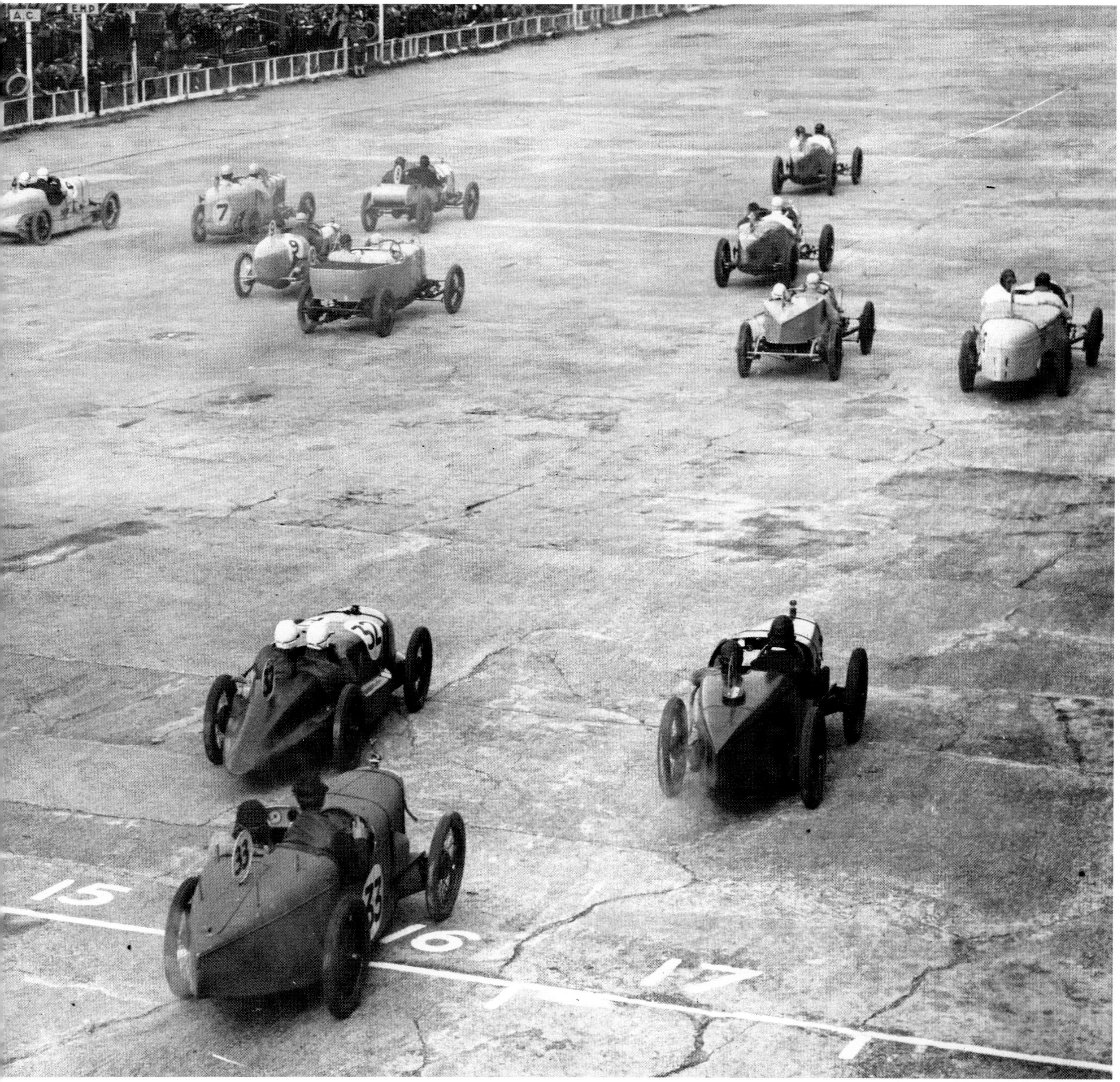
A.C.
15
16
17
7
9
33

La Coupe Florio poster (top left):

SAINT-BRIEUC - 17 Juillet 1927

PROGRAMME OFFICIEL · PRIX 3 FRANCS

LA COUPE FLORIO

GRANDE COURSE
INTERNATIONALE
AUTOMOBILE

Organisation Générale-Journal L'Ouest-Eclair
Pouvoir Sportif: Automobile Club des Côtes du Nord

Overleaf:

*Left: Approaching the Brooklands
test hill in a 1925 high-speed trial for light cars*

*Right: The Hon. Victor Bruce
with his AC en route for Monte Carlo*

*Inset: "To the Victors belong the spoils" –
the AC at Monte Carlo after winning the Rally*

Opposite page:

*Top: This is Jules Goux;
that is a type 35 Bugatti; the rest is Sicily*

*Bottom: The last GP Fiat,
the 1½ litre U12, raced once
in 1927, won easily, and was then scrapped*

*Top, left: The Sicilian audience may not
have seen a T37 Bugatti
engine before 1927. Had they seen a camera?*

*Top, right: Spurning the dust: immaculate
Varzi in Type 51 Bugatti for the Targa Florio*

*Bottom, left: Winner of the first
Mille Miglia, the OM was made in Brescia*

*Bottom, right: Low lightweights were
a French speciality in the 1100cc class.
This Amilcar is racing at Boulogne in 1928*

EN TOUS GENRES
Maurice LEFEBVRE
POÊLERIE
ÉLECTRICITÉ

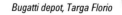

Bugatti depot, Targa Florio

own masonically proportioned way, and wherever roadholding and handling and braking and sheer artistic harmony mattered more than power and speed, there was most satisfaction in a Bugatti. It showed best in the Targa Florio; but in mainland Italy there came a new long-distance road race, for sports and touring cars to contest over a thousand old Roman miles, from Brescia to Rome and back again. Superb handling qualities brought an OM home as winner of the first Mille Miglia in 1927, but after that it was almost always an Alfa victory.

Often the winning car was tantamount to a GP machine with lights and mudguards, because GP rules continued to stipulate room for a riding mechanic even after 1925, when riding mechanics were forbidden. Outside impetuous impatient Italy, itching as it was to acquire the supremacy promised by its popular dictator, long-distance sports-car races were meant to develop really practical touring cars; the rules stipulated four seats, ballast to represent their occupants, and serious attention to lamps, hood, and fuel consumption.

85

The Tourist Trophy, revived in the Isle of Man in 1922, was meant to be such a race, but was to have so chequered a career that eventually only its name would survive intact, a race with no fixed address. The 1922 effort was poorly supported, notable only for the good showing of the new Bentleys which, running on Pirelli tyres in the pouring rain, won the team prize. The Bentley was

*Top: Frank Lockhart
in his "Stutz Black Hawk",
the Miller-engined car that should
have earned him a world record in 1928*

*Bottom: First with wings:
Fritz von Opel demonstrates rocket propulsion*

Top: Grandstands in the Targa Florio hills

Bottom: Adolf Rosenberger, brilliant amateur in a Mercedes-Benz on Klausen hill-climb, 1928. Later he was adviser/partner to Porsche, but had to quit (he was Jewish) when Hitler came to power

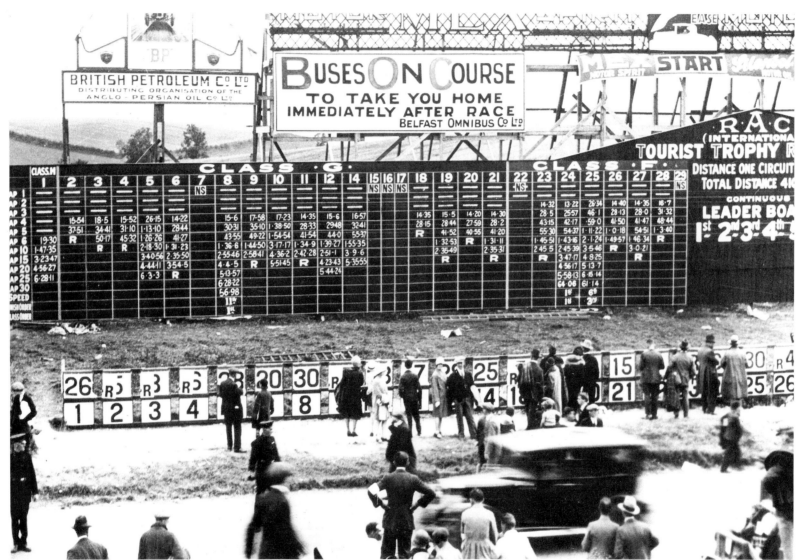

1928 TT

*Sir Malcolm Campbell's
Bugatti burnt out of the 1928 TT*

Traffic jam, 1929: start of the TT

The fastest Bentleys
had severe tyre problems in 1929 and 1930

Scuderia Ferrari al fresco,
with a lovely old German chain-hoist

to earn greater fame in the race that was born to greatness the following year, the Grand Prix d'Endurance des Vingt-quatre Heures du Mans.

Le Mans, for short. It started in 1923; a Bentley won in 1924, in 1927/8/9/30. Disappointing elsewhere, disastrous in business, the Bentley was worshipped solely because of its feats at Le Mans. Its drivers, 'the Bentley Boys', were society idols whose Mayfair parties were reported as gleefully as their racing successes.

Gifted drivers were given all the publicity they could take; and some were very gifted indeed. In the early twenties, Fiat driver Bordino was the fastest of them all; at the end of that decade, all Italy adored indomitable little Tazio Nuvolari, who came from fame as a motorcyclist to a blaze of glory as defender of the honour of the nation and, as often as not, of Alfa Romeo. He was lionized outside Italy, too; but there were some who looked askance at his colourful clothes and lifestyle, who doubted the drifting style he developed to save his brakes at the expense of his tyres and transmissions, and who admired the icy-cold precision and immaculate conduct of his arch rival Achille Varzi.

Some knew even better. There was a quiet young German who never seemed to strain his car, who was unbeatable in the rain, who could handle the biggest and clumsiest Mercedes-Benz so deftly as to give the agile little Bugattis a hard run for their money round the houses of Monte Carlo in the tight new 'race of a thousand corners', the Monaco GP. He alone could defy the apparent impossibility of defeating the Italians on their home ground in the Mille Miglia, as he did with a Mercedes-Benz in 1931; he alone could outdrive Nuvolari in an identical Alfa Romeo, as he did at Monaco in 1932, before waving the little Italian through to save his face and friendship. Rudolf Caracciola, despite physical pain and personal tragedy seldom revealed, was probably the best driver of them all, and in 1933 his greatest years were still ahead of him.

If he had much to endure, few had it easy. Times were hardest of all in Germany, but

*Main picture: Le Mans start, 1930:
Caracciola, Clement, Davis,
Kidston and others run to their cars*

*Far right: "Speed Six"
and "Blower 4½" – Bentleys, 1930*

*Left: Caracciola (Mercedes-Benz)
at the station hairpin in the 1929 Monaco GP*

*Right: The map of the Mille Miglia was
more probably imprinted
on Nuvolari's retinae than on his necktie*

Centre: Sicily, 1930: Varzi scores another Alfa Romeo victory in a P2

Below: There used to be a Concours de Confort in the Monte Carlo Rally. Here it is in 1929

Left, top to bottom:

*Nuvolari in a
1750 Alfa Romeo at Firenze, 1930*

*Brave chaps,
those press photographers, sitting on the
Brooklands track while the Bentleys hurtle by*

*A beautiful 1750 Alfa Romeo,
going beautifully with Caracciola at the wheel*

Centre, top to bottom:

*Lt Col Goldie Gardner,
more famous as a record-breaker,
readies his Amilcar for the 1930 Irish "GP"*

Newtownards Square during the 1930 TT

Nuvolari, 1930 TT winner in an Alfa Romeo

Right, top to bottom:

*Coming through
Comber in the 1930 TT, an Earl
(Howe) in a Mercedes-Benz
and a Baronet (Birkin) in a Bentley*

*Boris Ivanowski was Russia's
best driver. He came third at
Le Mans in 1931 in this Mercedes-Benz.
Behind him is Brisson in a Stutz*

*Clustered around an early 8C-2300,
the men of the Alfa Romeo team in 1931*

everywhere had been hit by the shockwave which radiated from the Wall Street Crash in October 1929. The slump took men's fortunes, men took their lives, and motor racing – which always took a lot of money – suddenly took a lower order of priority wherever it was not bolstered by political or desperately commercial support. Rules were often ignored: those who could still race drove whatever they had, and the racing was often more interesting as a result.

They were great days, because there was not too much happening; and everything that happened mattered. The cars were as classically ordered as the architecture of old Greece, as formal in structure as a sonata. Their long engines sent roasting heat into their cockpits, while as much of the driver as could be suffered to protrude into the open air was battered by wind and weather. At least the barrage of stones grew less, and the dust abated: the friable water-bound surfaces of old had proved unable to endure motor traffic, and assorted methods of top-dressing made the roads less wrinkled, less likely to break down and furrow, as the 'twenties gave way to the 'thirties. The frightening plumes of dust once tracing the course of every car had vanished, and now there was a wonderful haze of voided exhaust, the intoxicating aphrodisiac miasma of scorched castor oil and burnt benzol hanging long in the emptied air where the blue song of a straight eight had rippled so briefly.

Not all events caused drivers and cars to work up such a sweat. Hillclimbs, sprints, modest club races scattered in a multitude of compact courses all over Europe, most of them were brief, and few called for more time and fuel than would empty a weekend's wallet. Yet it was possible to drive desperately for a week and never know better than the numbing cold which nailed knees rigid and gripped eyeballs immobile in their sockets: the

Centre: In 1933 starting grids
were still smoky, as here at Monaco

Top, left: Caracciola

Top, right: Hall waves team-mate
Nuvolari past to win the 1933 TT

Below, centre: Stuck

Overleaf:

*Left: The last vintage:
Type 59 Bugattis for Varzi and Dreyfus, 1933*

*Right: The Hotchkiss
was always a good Monte Carlo Rally car.
This is a 1933 competitor*

Centre: Building Cobb's Napier-Railton

*Below: A Napier Lion aero engine in
a robust and well-made chassis, John Cobb's
car was the fastest ever around Brooklands*

Monte Carlo Rally preceded the interior heater
by a considerable margin.

Revived in 1924, the rally expanded to take in
more starting points, with extra marks given to
those who started from the more difficult places;
1931 was the first year when anyone got through
from Athens within the time allowed. It was also the
year when Sir Malcolm Campbell began a run of
five world speed records with his Bluebirds.

Thirteen times since the war, the land speed
record had been raised from the 131.7 mph at
which the Blitzen Benz had left it in 1910. A Fiat had
been the last to set the record on an ordinary road,
at 146 mph in 1924; after that, it was done on the
sands of Pendine and Daytona, frequently and by
the smallest possible margin because it had
become a business rewarded by advertising fees
each time the record was broken. The only
contender of any real merit was the only refined
car among brutes, the super-slim Miller-engined
windslipper which should with just 3 magically
tuned litres have taken young Frank Lockhart to
225 mph in 1928, but instead took him to his death.
In 1932 Campbell took an aero-engined megatherion
to that same Florida beach and exceeded 250 mph
for the first time on land.

The press was duly impressed. Six years later it
would scarcely comment when Caracciola went
faster than that on a two-lane Autobahn…

BIGGER BILLING

The pyramid grew at base and apex: the spread of the sport became much greater, but it was harder than ever to reach the top. A new Grand Prix formula, supposed to restore sanity, instead proved to goad technology, the Germans spending and winning on behalf of Nazidom. The speed, the power, the noise, and the propaganda, were all without precedent.

Nobody else could compete; so everybody else went off and enjoyed the sport elsewhere. At Le Mans, at Brooklands, at Indianapolis; converging on Monte Carlo, circling Sicily, criss-crossing Italy; up a Cotswold hill, or down a tramlined Manx street, cars of almost all descriptions and drivers of sometimes indescribable character gave the sport of this period wonderful variety, and perhaps unmatched charm.

Terrifically stylish though these years were, they did not lack seriousness. The cars which were doing most of the winning were beginning to look decidedly modern – and that was by no means just a matter of styling.

1934 - 1941

Above: Despite the new German
might, the old Alfa Romeo of
Louis Chiron (here chasing Caracciola)
won the 1934 French GP at Montlhèry

Centre: Team manager
Neubauer confers with Caracciola
in a record-breaking roofed racer, 1934

Below, right: Montlhèry 1934

Main picture:
Auto-Unions on a there-and-back course

Inset: Auto-Union
have their first taste of GP racing

Overleaf:

Left: ERAs flank Staniland's
Multi-Union (an Alfa-based 'special')
and Bira's ex-Whitney Straight Maserati

Inset: Lea-Francis and Talbot at Brooklands

Right: Indianapolis 1934

Overleaf:

Left: The dirt of a thousand miles

Inset: MG in Mille Miglia, 1934

Right: Perrot's 1934 Delahaye:
the French were always good with lights

Opposite page:
Type 59 Bugatti, last of the blue blood

Top: Nuvolari regularly clipped this
corner in the 1933 TT, which he won for MG

Centre: 1934 TT: Lagonda and Riley

Bottom: Chain-drive Frazer Nash
leads Singer into Dundonald hairpin

The road beckons long and straight across the
Marne fields; the tyres bite as the car straightens
out of the hairpin; the accelerator pedal plumbs its
noisy depths. In the briefest of paroxysms, bottom
gear reaches the limit of its range at 80 mph.
Second gear flings the car to 98, third carries the
rush to 134. Each shift sounds instantaneous, yet
the next always sounds faster, and fourth gear
prolongs the push to 156 mph. Fifth gear now, a rare
luxury which brings discomfort: the wind is no
longer deflected adequately by the tiny aero screen
ahead, but comes tearing at the face, clawing the
cheeks' flesh back in hideous grimace, battering at
the tightly-fitting edge of the linen helmet, menacing
the moulded fit of the goggles. The road rises, falls,
reveals the onset of another corner and the need to
relent at 190 mph.

This is the French GP at Reims in 1939. This is a
V12 Mercedes-Benz, its doubly supercharged 3-litre
engine drinking a gallon of alcohol, acetone, nitro-
benzene and ether every three miles and making
480 bhp available to Hermann Lang, fastest and
most tigerish driver in the world, lapping at a speed
not to be matched for another twelve years.

This is what it had come to, six years after Hitler
had come to power. It was fabulous, terrific racing
of furious intent and febrile rivalry – between just
two teams, Auto-Union with the engine behind the
driver and Mercedes-Benz with the driver behind
the engine. One or other was sure to win, and either
way the German propaganda machine was happy
to continue financing and publicising them.

It was superbly managed – and stage-managed
– and impeccably professional. It demonstrated
beyond question the extraordinary potential of
advanced technology when combined with
powerful motivation. It left any other competitors –
those who still believed that this was a sport, or
something similarly amateurish and trivial – having
their own private race, somewhere trailing in the
dim and distant rear. And it had been going on like
that, ever more emphatically and incontestably,
since 1934.

A new formula governed the construction of GP
cars from the beginning of that season. Dismayed

VIII MILLE MIGLIA
1° ASSOLUTO ACHILLE VARZI

Centre: Early preparations
in the Mercedes-Benz pits, Monaco

Below, right:
Maseratis in charge at Modena, 1935

Mercedes-Benz 1935

Opposite:

Main picture: ERA in the Isle of Man

Inset, top: Bugatti and ERA in the Isle of Man

Inset, bottom: The Isle of Man, where Englishmen could race in the streets

Centre: Notably durable and stable, the 1½ litre Aston Martin did very well at Le Mans in '35 – but not this one

Below, left: Le Mans 1935

Below, right: Lagonda winning at Le Mans in 1935, the year in which newcomer Fontes had a meteoric season before leaving motor-racing for aviation. His co-driver Hindmarsh was a test pilot

INTERNATIONAL
MANNIN · MOAR · RACE
DOUGLAS 1934

BUGATTI
Type 57 S

2 RECORDS DE 24 HEURES
Record du monde et
24 H LE MANS

la seule voiture
FRANÇAISE
sur route
et sur piste
Record international
MONTHLERY

Centre: Ernst von Delius in the V16 Auto-Union

Below, left: So successful was
Richard Seaman in this 1927 Delage in
the 1½ litre races of 1936 that he was
invited to drive for Mercedes-Benz in 1937

Below, right: Nuvolari (V12 Alfa Romeo)
in hot pursuit of a straight-8 Mercedes-Benz

Centre: The 1936 French GP
was for sports cars. Autographs of
Bugatti and Wimille attest the winner

Nuvolari

What Nuvolari wore

by the power and speed, and even more by the
incorrigibility, of the fastest cars of 1932, the
legislators had decided that sanity might best be
restored by imposing a 750 kg weight limit for the
cars (without driver, tyres, or fluids) and, to deter
dangerous fragility, setting a minimum distance of
500 km for each race. Hitler, already a motoring
enthusiast when he came to power, confounded
them: he saw the value of motor racing as an
advertisement for the superiority of Nazi Germany,
and goaded his industry into proof.

Dominion did not come forthwith. The valour
and virtuosity of Nuvolari sometimes humbled the
Germans, but such feats grew rapidly less frequent.
Calm Caracciola led the Mercedes-Benz team
through two increasingly successful seasons,
backed and sometimes challenged by the wildly
tempestuous Manfred von Brauchitsch (nephew of
the Field Marshal) and supported by various others.
Lang's chance would come later; at this stage he
was a team mechanic, who knew precisely how
much more punishment the cars could take than
the team drivers were cautioned to give them.

Stuck opened for Auto-Union, but it was seen to
be a very tricky car to drive: everybody said it was
because of the rear engine, but that was because
they did not understand the niceties of independent
suspension. The real reason was that the car's
designer, Dr Porsche, did not understand them
any better. Stuck's place was taken by a young
motorcycle racer, Bernd Rosemeyer, who knew no
better nor cared: he had never raced any other car,
and for all he knew they were all like this – so he
flung it about with Aryan abandon, and by 1936 the
6-litre Auto-Union was doing better than the
Mercedes-Benz.

Roles were reversed in 1937, when Mercedes-
Benz issued a new car, so sweet in its behaviour
that it could deploy more straight-eight power than

Left to right:

Rosemeyer at full tilt

Chaos on the harbour front at Monaco, 1936

Monaco 1936: starting grid places used to be allocated by lot

Art flourished in relief and in enamel
on trophies, medals and (very fashionably)
the heraldry of club badges displayed
on car-fronts

any racing car had ever had, more than any racing car ever would have for another forty years. That car, and the V12 which succeeded it when a new formula took effect in 1938 to cut engines down in size and power, was so convincing that racing cars continued to be made in its image for as long as engines remained ahead of drivers.

'The fathers have eaten sour grapes,' cried Ezekiel, 'and the children's teeth are set on edge.' Italy hit on a neat way to exclude the Germans, proclaiming a 1½-litre engine limit for all races held on Italian soil – which then included the blisteringly fast Tripoli GP. Maserati had some little cars which could get along quite fast when streamlined; Alfa Romeo confected an exquisite new 1½-litre straight eight (half of their ill-conceived 3-litre GP car) and made it immortal when they christened it Alfetta.

Stylish straight-armed Dr Farina brought the Alfetta into sixth place behind the Germans in the fast and cursive Berne GP, so it looked likely that Italy might have a winner at Tripoli – especially since the news of the limit was posted as late as possible. With only weeks to go when they heard about it, Mercedes-Benz built a pair of 1½ litre engines, put them into chassis practically identical to their 3-litre cars, and beat the Italians fair and square.

That was surely the firmest (and most expensive) put-down in motor racing history, and the French were not going to risk anything similar. They had long lost touch with single-seaters; they simply turned as many of their races as possible into sports-car events, in which their big blue blasters by Bugatti, Delage, Delahaye and Talbot would brook no nonsense from anybody – not even from rabid Alfa Romeo, nor even from clean and devastatingly modern BMW.

The same applied to rallies. The heady Alpine, a Bugatti playground lately invaded with success by the chain-driven Frazer Nash from funny old England, was transferred to Switzerland and then dropped altogether. The punishing Marathon de la Route, strictly a Belgian race on open roads from Liège to Rome and back non-stop, was dominated by French cars. So was that Hotchkiss speciality,

Top, left:
Quick-lift jacks under a Type 59 Bugatti

Top, right: Bad weather at Brooklands

Centre strip: Supreme in '37, led
by Caracciola (far left), the Mercedes-Benz
team could retyre and
refuel the 600 horsepower car in 40 seconds

Drivers, left to right:

'Bira' – HRH Prince Birabongse of Siam

Manfred von Brauchitsch

Jean-Pierre Wimille
early in his career, probably in 1933

Bernd Rosemeyer

Hermann Lang

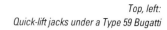

Above, left: The mother of heroes; Carolina Losi gave six motoring sons to her engine-driver husband, Rodolfo Maserati

Above, right: Horse-breeder Ettore Bugatti demonstrates a chair he designed

Centre, top: Start of the 1937 Vanderbilt Cup, with no Americans in the leading septet

Board-track, USA

the Monte Carlo Rally.

Funny old England still treated motoring as a sport. International events were open to all comers; national events were progressively dominated by the ERA, a Riley-based racing car built in sparse numbers by a tiny country company, with joint proprietor Raymond Mays proving himself the best of British drivers, especially up the hills where he had starred since the vintage years. Like English motor racing itself, the ERA was for gifted and gilded amateurs – bandleader Billy Cotton, whose acute ear saved him many a burst engine, or Siamese Prince Birabongse whose impassive elegance and unfailing precision gave Mays many a close run for his money. Bira was eagerly sought by professional teams, and as eagerly went in search of competent cars: he did well with the Maserati formerly raced by a fine American amateur, Whitney Straight.

Amateurism was fine, in England. In the USA, some semblance of professionalism was essential, but nobody else had quite the same brand of competence as Mauri Rose. Piling up experience since 1927 on the half-mile dirt tracks, and graduating to the one-milers five years later, he was at the same time a development engineer for Hupmobile. By the time he moved to Chevrolet he was already an Indianapolis driver, and remained one for fifteen races in a row; but he took it in his stride. Other drivers spent a month in preparation for the annual 500 Miles race, but not he: one weekend to practise, one to qualify, and then back to his regular job until the day before the race. On the day, Rose was almost always on the leader board, though his first of three wins was not until 1941. Nevertheless he was national driving champion in 1936, and also the first American home behind Europe's best (Nuvolari won in an Alfa Romeo) when the Vanderbilt Cup was revived on the new Roosevelt Raceway in New York state.

Within a couple of years, the Nazis had the Vanderbilt event wrapped up too. America reeled, but more shocks were to come: Indy was conquered, two years in a row, by a foreign car, a Maserati. At least the driver, Wilbur Shaw, was

PRICE: ONE SHILLING

MIDLAND AUTOMOBILE CLUB.

OFFICIAL HANDBOOK FOR 1935
AND PROGRAMME
OF THE
30TH ANNIVERSARY
INTERNATIONAL OPEN HILL CLIMB
AT
SHELSLEY WALSH
On SATURDAY, MAY 18th, 1935, at 1 p.m.
HELD UNDER THE RULES OF A.I.A.C.R. AND R.A.C. PERMIT No. 129

The Motor For the FIRST
FULL REPORT
of this event see next Tuesday's issue.
PRICE 6d.

Previous page:

*Left: The S-bend, favourite
spot for Shelsley Walsh spectators*

Right: Shelsley Walsh 1937

*Inset, left: Beautifully made and very
highly supercharged, the 750cc Austin single-
seater did 4 miles per gallon of sprint fuel*

*Inset, right: 30/98 Vauxhall
at the bottom of Shelsley Walsh hillclimb*

*Centre: Four tyres
and forty gallons in forty seconds*

Strip, top to bottom

Delage 3-litre at Donington

*Winner of the touring class and fourth overall
in the '37 Mille Miglia: the 6C2300 Alfa Romeo*

*National styles in 1937: BMW from
Germany, Delahaye from France, and Singer
not quite at home in the TT at Donington*

Nuvolari in the 1938 Auto-Union

Below: Livorno, 1937

Strip, top to bottom:

Caracciola, 1938

Pescara, 1938

Caracciola at Reims, 1938

The streamlined Lancia Aprilia
(body by Pinin Farina) in the Targa Abruzzi, 1938

an American.

Not all American racing was focused on the Brickyard of Indiana. The nation never had any central organisation governing competition motoring, and there were always sturdily independent Americans who would have had nothing to do with anything so officious. In the southern states there was racing of 'outlaw' status on half-mile dirt tracks, in deviously modified sedans muscled by good ol' boys who learned all manner of driving tricks running moonshine down from the hills in the prohibition era.

It was rough, it was hilarious, it was good-natured, and it was in due course to develop into NASCAR races for blindingly fast pseudo-stock sedans packed fender-to-fender on banked concrete ovals – or, if anyone got out of line, parked fender-to-fender somewhere near the edge.

Before that could happen, we had to have another war after all. The Germans were still racing a few hours after hostilities were formally begun, at Beograd for the 1939 Jugoslav GP (Nuvolari won for Auto-Union, which made a pleasant change), but everybody was guaranteed a clear passage home afterwards. Italy kept out of the war until the following year, which allowed time for an Alfetta to win her Tripoli GP, but also allowed a BMW to win her reduced-scale Mille Miglia. America kept out until the year after that, which allowed an American car (with the latest Offenhauser version of Leo Goossen's lovely engine) to recover the Indy title.

Thereafter, there were no excuses.

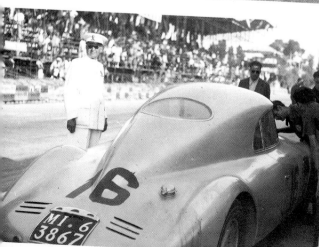

Above: Coming off
the banking at Berlin's fast AVUS track

Right: Twin tyres
for traction at twisty Crystal Palace

Opposite, inset: This Mille Miglia special
BMW was ready with fuel injection in 1940.
In the event, carburettors were used instead

Main picture: Short circuits had to
be devised at Brooklands, to introduce
some corners and relieve the monotony

Centre: Frazer Nash
(i.e. right-hand-drive)
BMWs in the 1939 RAC Rally

Strip, left to right:

Cross-country trials, Germany

Waiting for the Le Mans start, 1939

For a Brooklands winner
one needed a really big flag

Aviatrix Amy Johnson (centre)
and Mrs McEvoy check in
at the Folkestone control during
the 1939 Monte Carlo Rally. The car is a Ford V8

Waiting for the Channel ferry,
a 1939 Monte Carlo Rally
driver snatches precious sleep

Below: Modern, traditional
and ideological art all flourished
in the design of motoring trophies.
This assortment is from the Nuvolari collection

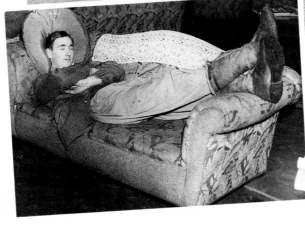

Main picture: Fastest ever on a public
road, the low-drag 5½ litre V12 Mercedes-Benz

Inset, left: Cross-country trials
in Germany were not always military,
but they looked it. The car is a DKW

Inset, right: Standards of dress do vary in trials

Below, left: Maserati on
the Nurburgring weighbridge, 1939

Below, right:
Team-manager Neubauer shepherds
Lang and his V12 Mercedes-Benz to the start

NEW STARTS

In the austerity of post-war Europe, the sport was reseeded with an urgency that was more procreational than recreational. In the prosperity of post-war America, motor racing was still more social than rational, but the passing of isolationism led to the coming of European cars and a growing awareness of how great a role the USA might eventually play.

Even more phenomenal growth was registered in Britain, where the sport spread like wildfire. All over the world, and especially in England, events were taking place at all levels. A golden age of Grand Prix racing reflected the lustre of famous makers and formidable drivers; competitions for sports cars and touring cars, for home-built specials and humdrum family saloons, saw multitudes polishing new skills.

Some of the shine was knocked off at Le Mans by the most ghastly tragedy in motoring history; but that history was due for revision anyway. A few cocky newcomers were dismissing old traditions with new theories, bidding to turn the whole business back to front…

1945 - 1958

Berne 1947

After the war to end all wars, the war to end all hope; and after that, years of austerity, of rehabilitation, of return, and of recreation.

It was a measure of how deeply the enthusiasm for motor sport had been impressed on people in the late 1930s that the survivors should have been so anxious to revive the sport as quickly as they could. The man who won the first post-war race, eloquently entitled Grand Prix des Prisonniers and held in the Bois de Boulogne, Paris, in 1945, was lucky to have survived. Several of his friends in the French Resistance, famous racing drivers such as Williams and Benoist, had been caught and killed; but Jean-Pierre Wimille, victor at Le Mans in 1939, won what were probably his most grateful laurels, at the wheel of the Bugatti in which he had come second to Nuvolari in the 1936 Vanderbilt race.

Bugatti was nevertheless a spent force. As the resources of racing were anxiously numbered, it emerged that there were Alfettas, there were Talbots, there were ERAs and Maseratis, and quite a lot of sports cars still around and ready. In 1946 little race meetings, hillclimbs, sprints and rallies sprang up all over western Europe. England had lost Brooklands, but a private park or a disused airfield would serve for a sprint, perhaps shared with motorcycles. Hermann Lang won the Ruhestein hillclimb in the very BMW that had beaten the Italians in their makeshift Mille Miglia of 1940. And in Italy a big iron-willed man who had entered the first two cars of his own construction in that race now set about making a modern racer to bear his own name, Ferrari.

He was not a young man now; but he never had been, even in his early days driving for CMN in the 1919 Targa Florio. He had ever after been associated with Alfa Romeo, and was responsible for their racing team from 1929 to 1938, by which time they had come under state control. The cars he built in 1940 were made of Fiat parts; the new ones had elegant little V12 engines designed by Colombo, who had designed the Alfetta, but they still incorporated a lot of Fiat parts. They gave a lot of trouble, but also a lot of satisfaction, and when a pretty barchetta-bodied two-seater won the first

Franco Cortese rockfisting the '48 Ferrari

Below: Level pegging: small engines with superchargers have long fought big ones without, and still do – but never with such drama as when Alfa Romeo fought Ferrari

Nice GP, mostly Maseratis

*First race for
a GP Ferrari, in the centre of Torino in 1948*

Below, left: Mays at his best:
D-type ERA at Craigantlet hillclimb

Below, right:
The lightweight HRG team for Spa and Le Mans

Centre: Alberto Ascari

What Ascari carried

*Opposite: 4CLT/48 or
'San Remo' Maserati, first post-war
car to have two-stage supercharging*

*Left: Lago Talbot,
last of the big French beauties*

*Above: Prototype
demonstration: Mays in the first BRM*

Right: Another Alpine Gold Cup for skier Ian Appleyard

Below, right: Il Cabezon defies the bullfighters of Milano

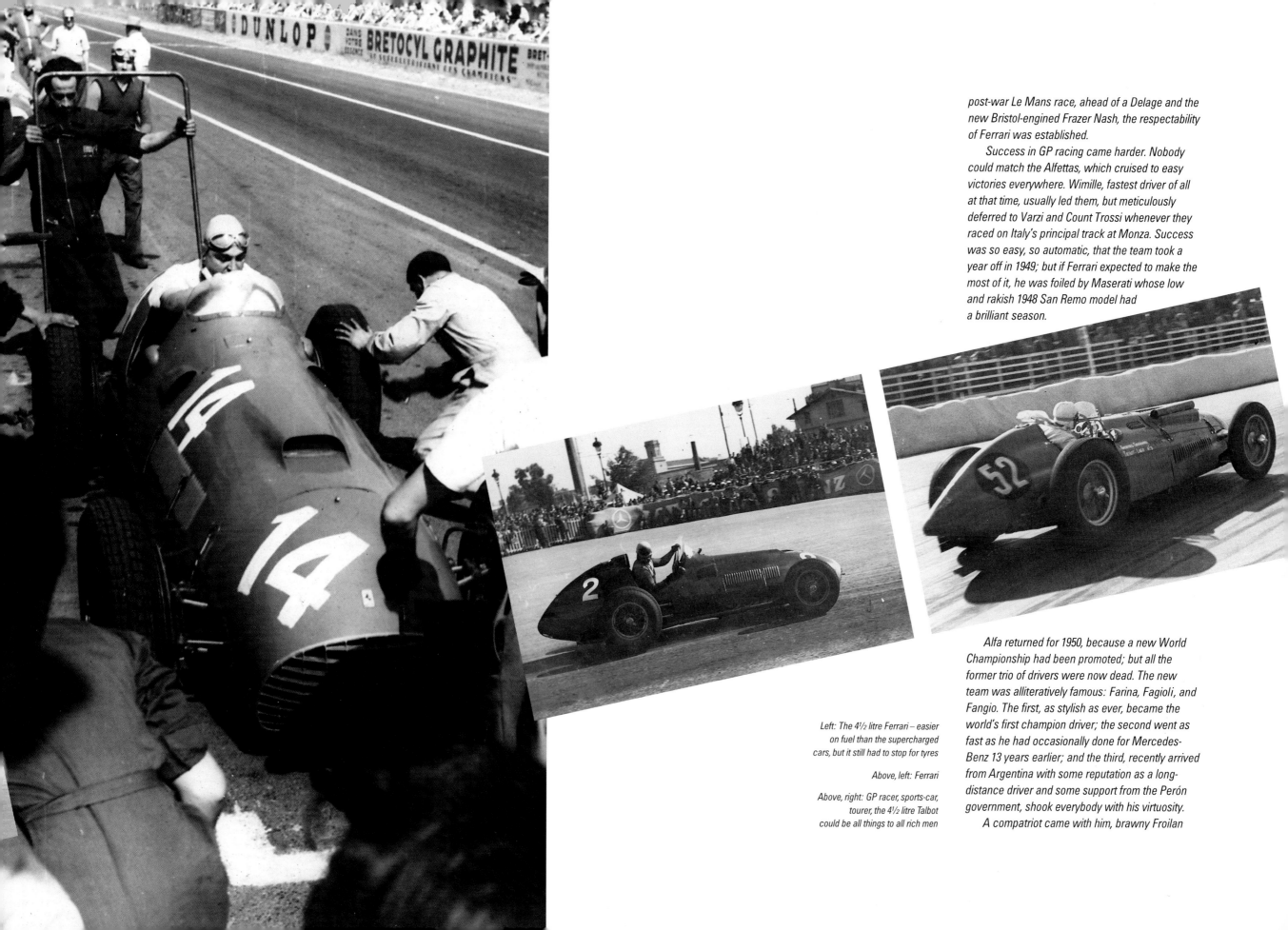

post-war Le Mans race, ahead of a Delage and the new Bristol-engined Frazer Nash, the respectability of Ferrari was established.

Success in GP racing came harder. Nobody could match the Alfettas, which cruised to easy victories everywhere. Wimille, fastest driver of all at that time, usually led them, but meticulously deferred to Varzi and Count Trossi whenever they raced on Italy's principal track at Monza. Success was so easy, so automatic, that the team took a year off in 1949; but if Ferrari expected to make the most of it, he was foiled by Maserati whose low and rakish 1948 San Remo model had a brilliant season.

Left: The 4½ litre Ferrari – easier on fuel than the supercharged cars, but it still had to stop for tyres

Above, left: Ferrari

Above, right: GP racer, sports-car, tourer, the 4½ litre Talbot could be all things to all rich men

Alfa returned for 1950, because a new World Championship had been promoted; but all the former trio of drivers were now dead. The new team was alliteratively famous: Farina, Fagioli, and Fangio. The first, as stylish as ever, became the world's first champion driver; the second went as fast as he had occasionally done for Mercedes-Benz 13 years earlier; and the third, recently arrived from Argentina with some reputation as a long-distance driver and some support from the Perón government, shook everybody with his virtuosity.

A compatriot came with him, brawny Froilan

Below: Sidney Allard sets
a new sports-car record
for the sea-front kilometre sprint at Brighton

Left to right:

Alfa Romeo at Monza, 1950

Last of the blown straight-eights

Top: Early V-twin Cooper
on the inside line, A-type Connaught outside

Bottom: Alfette, in line ahead, as usual

King George VI meets the drivers at Silverstone

Goggles and helmet: A first-class driver in
pre-war days, Luigi Fagioli, kept his form when
linen helmets gave way to crash-hats

Gonzales; and it was he who, at the wheel of a big unsupercharged Ferrari designed by an outstanding newcomer, Aurelio Lampredi, at last beat the Alfettas in 1951. It was a titanic battle, fought at Silverstone under a broiling sun; yet Farina and Ascari, the latter in another Ferrari, were left in the shade as the two Argentinians tore at the tarmac and tore up the history books. On that unforgettable day, they were writing another: the long reign of the supercharged engine, begun by Fiat in 1923, was over. By the end of the year, a new Grand Prix formula had been written, stipulating unsupercharged engines of 2½ litres, with two years of low-key races to fill the interval needed for preparation.

Had the BRM not been such a bitter disappointment, this might not have happened. The brainchild of Raymond Mays, it was to have been a British world-beater, the combined product of all the skills of British industry – but that involved too many cooks, and the broth was spoilt. Designer Berthon effectively created a cross between the 1939 Mercedes-Benz and a wartime Alfa Romeo design by the Spanish intellectual Ricart. Its 16 tiny force-fed cylinders uttered the most captivating music that ever monopolized eardrums – and that, prima facie, was its only achievement.

In retrospect, it achieved far more. By his tireless campaigning to persuade British industry and the British media of the importance of motor racing, so as to justify the investment the BRM demanded, Mays actually persuaded the British public to become the sport's most enthusiastic supporters. He had begun to educate their appetite in 1946; by 1949 they were insatiable.

In the absence of any joy from the BRM, they rejoiced over the lovely new Jaguar XK120 in 1949, revelled in its conquest of the Alpine Rally in the

*Above: Gonzales (Maserati)
on the Monza cobbles, 1952*

Left: J.F. Gonzales

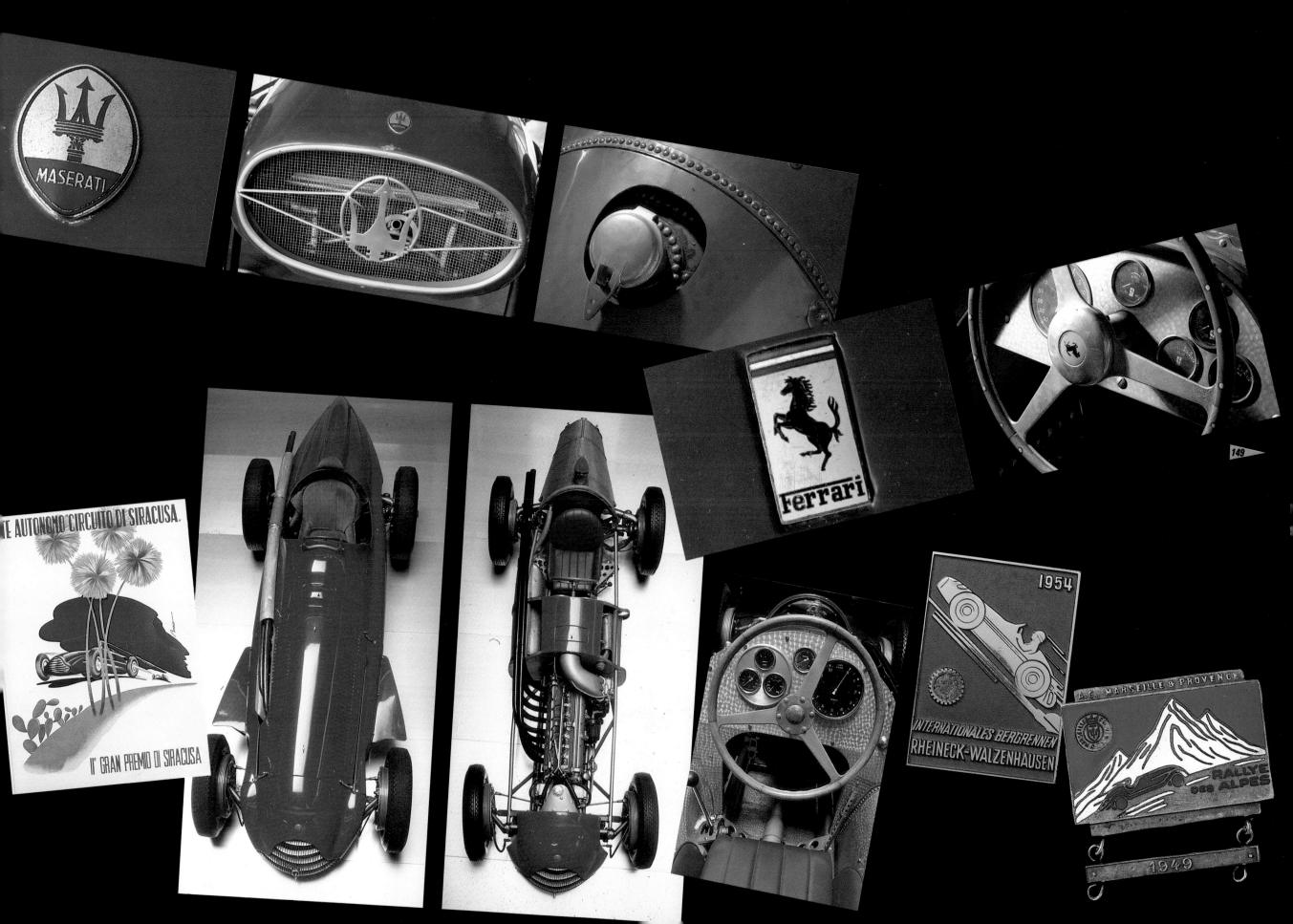

MASERATI

ferrari

149

E AUTONOMO CIRCUITO DI SIRACUSA

II° GRAN PREMIO DI SIRACUSA

1954

INTERNATIONALES BERGRENNEN
RHEINECK-WALZENHAUSEN

A.G. MARSEILLE & PROVENCE

RALLYE DES ALPES

1949

*Fangio, trying
very hard indeed at Silverstone in '51*

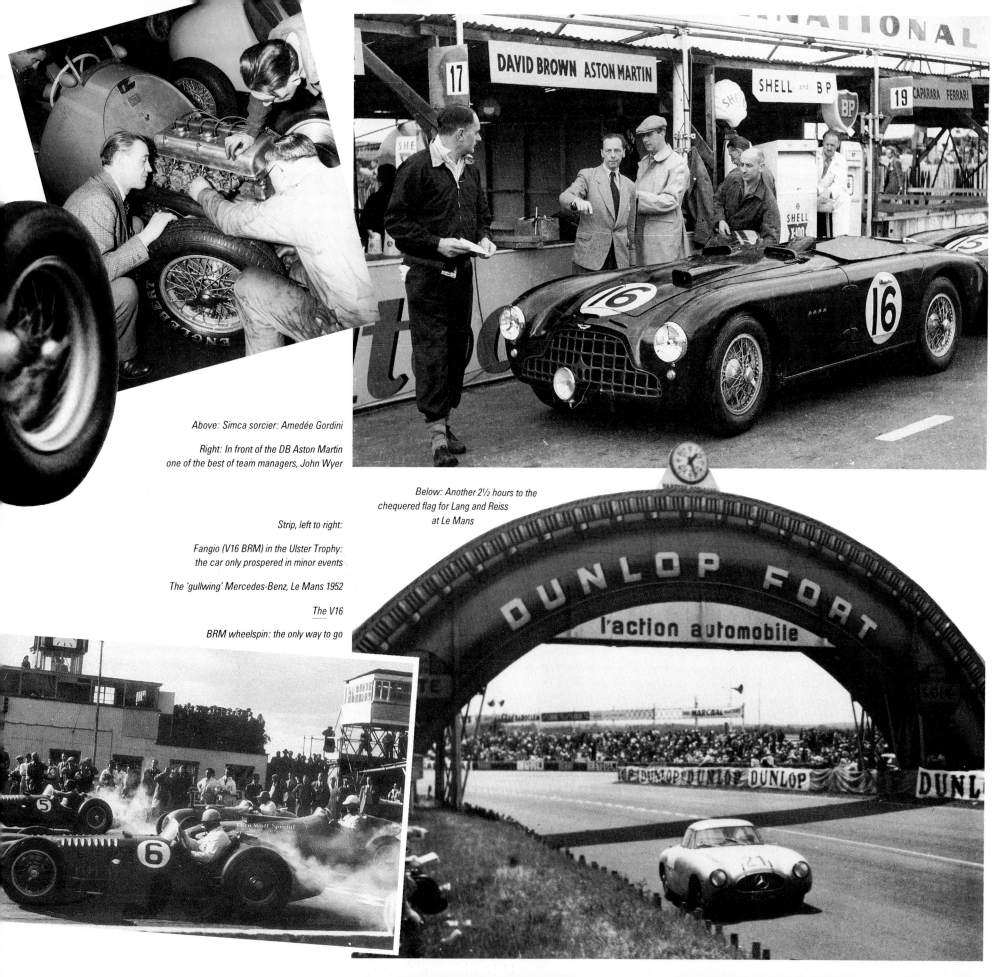

Above: Simca sorcier: Amedée Gordini

Right: In front of the DB Aston Martin one of the best of team managers, John Wyer

Strip, left to right:

Fangio (V16 BRM) in the Ulster Trophy: the car only prospered in minor events

The 'gullwing' Mercedes-Benz, Le Mans 1952

The V16

BRM wheelspin: the only way to go

Below: Another 2½ hours to the chequered flag for Lang and Reiss at Le Mans

following year, gave thanks for the good show by Aston Martin at Le Mans, and were deliriously happy when the C-type Jaguar won at Le Mans in 1951. At home, every empty airfield, any available park drive, whatsoever leaf-moulded hill or grassy bank that could be borrowed, rented, or trespassed upon, was pressed into service for races, sprints, hillclimbs, and those peculiarly English and particularly amiable events known as sporting trials (officially) and mudplugging (in the vernacular).

Cars were expensive, and new cars almost unobtainable, such was the pressure of the export drive. Yet the people – the common people, not just the wealthy and aristocratic whose preserve the sport had once been – wanted to drive. They devised a plan for cheap racing, involving simple little home-made chassis powered by half-litre motorcycle engines, and before long there were shoals of these stuttering megaphoning miniatures minnowing around all the circuits. Soon it was clear that the best layout involved a rear engine; soon after, it was apparent that the best chassis was a Cooper; and soon again there emerged from the pack a most uncommon young man, his habitual victories showing him eminently capable and exceedingly astute, named Stirling Moss.

The phenomenon of the 'fifties and the darling of the popular press, Moss was the greatest driver in the age of world championships never to be world champion. None could question his ability, and his worth was confirmed when he was invited to join the Mercedes-Benz team for the 1955 season, second to none but the only man fit to be his master, team-leader Juan Manuel Fangio.

The German firm, which its directors had declared no longer existent in 1945, had returned to sports-car racing in 1952 after four years of rapid resurgence. Only a few events were entered, the few that were of the utmost commercial importance: Le Mans, the Mille Miglia, the (sports-car) Grand Prix de Berne, and the still fairly new Carrera PanAmericana – a four-day thrash down the length of Mexico. The car was sensational, the gullwing-doored 300SL coupé, a streamlined aluminium envelope packed with innovations and

151

Opposite: Zandvoort, 1953:
Ascari was at his best when in the lead

Above: Fangio in the V16 BRM at Albi in 1953

Centre, top: '53 pit stop, Le Mans

Centre, bottom:
Amateur in the best sense,
Cunningham finished well at Le Mans

Right, top: A wet Mille Miglia for Farina

Right, bottom: President Peron toasts sweat-
soaked drivers after the 1953 Argentinian GP

Above: The Jaguar team en route for Le Mans

Centre: 1955: Hamilton, Jaguar, Reims

*Centre: A Bristol 450 splashes by,
as Jaguar's 1954 D-type
is readied for a fresh driver*

*Below: Consistent winner of class
and team awards at Reims
and Le Mans, the Bristol 450
was nicknamed 'the fighter pilot's delight'*

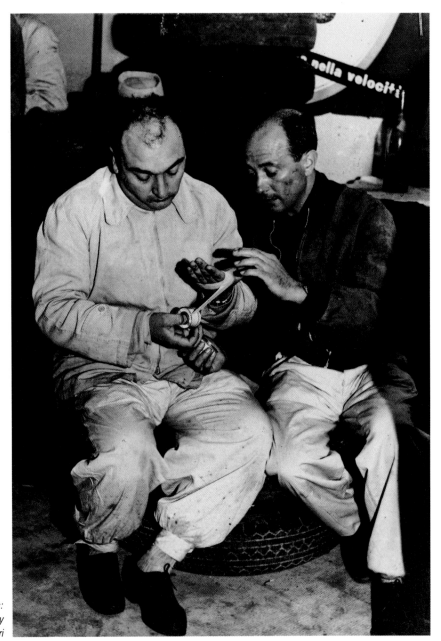

Night at Le Mans:
Gonzales bandages his hand, battered by
hours of gear changing in the brutal 4.9 Ferrari

Fangio's sister Alfa, starting at 6.02 am, finished second in the '53 Mille Miglia – with only one front wheel still steering!

Beautiful engineering: Connaught, 1953

able to outrun a C-type Jaguar.

It did just that in the Mille Miglia, finishing second to one of the Ferraris that won it six times in a row from 1948. Mercedes-Benz won the other three events, and then set about designing a GP car for the 1954-7 seasons. It too would be packed solid with scientific innovations: it should begin with 250 bhp and streamlining, and end at the expiration of the formula's term with 400 bhp and four-wheel drive. It would be tested to perfection by Rudolph Uhlenhaut, the Chief Designer who was also competent to drive it at racing speeds around the reeling Nurburgring, the knotted 17-miles test track which also served as the world's most taxing racetrack.

The debut of that car, at Reims in 1954, was absolutely authoritative. Ascari simply blew up his Ferrari trying to keep the two silver arrows in sight. Some subsequent races saw mistakes made, but at the end of the year Fangio had won often enough to claim his second World Championship. He was not without opposition, most worthily from a very fast and unusual V8 Lancia; but, with Moss supporting him, Mercedes-Benz won nearly everything in 1955, and Fangio was champion a third time – and looking for a job.

There would be no more racing for Mercedes-Benz. Their plans were shelved. They had been running two-seaters developed from the GP car in the major sports-car events, and Moss had won an imperishably famous Mille Miglia in one of the greatest drives of his life. At Le Mans, despite spirited opposition from Hawthorn in a Jaguar, the team was strongly placed, as always under the meticulous control of their formidable manager Neubauer, when with a bump and a searing flash everything went horribly wrong.

Some things are better forgotten, but the faces which saw what happened are memorable enough. Bristol were filming from their pits, the camera aimed down the road towards the corner beyond; when the bump registered, every face turned towards the lens, and every face was the mask of tragedy. There had been a minor traffic melee as cars came in and out of the pits, and one of them

*Left: Monza '54: The Ferrari is just
an expansion of the earlier Formula 2 car*

*Right: Monza '55: Ferrari now had
the V8 Lancia to deploy, as well as
the Supersqualo 4-cylinder Ferrari beyond*

*Below, top:
Silver fox and young lion: Piero Taruffi, Phil Hill*

Below, bottom: Conference: Ascari and Ferrari

Left to right:

*Alfette in preparation:
properly booted first, and then spurred…*

*Slipper-bodied version
of the '54 Mercedes-Benz*

*At Daimler-Benz, even the painting
of the numbers must be done properly*

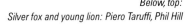

had hung its tail an instant too long in the path of the third Mercedes-Benz, coming flat out with French guest Pierre Levegh at the wheel. That tail served as a launching ramp: Levegh's car leaped into the air, smashed onto the earth bank separating the road from the public enclosure, and exploded into the crowd. Eighty-three were killed.

At 2 o'clock in the morning, with Fangio in the lead, Mercedes-Benz withdrew from the race; but poor Hawthorn was ordered to continue to a miserable victory. The public outrage was all that could be expected: some races were cancelled for the season, some forever, and everywhere safety provisions were questioned, fences erected, trees felled, and memories whitewashed. Two years later, the Marquis de Portago crashed his Ferrari into the Mille Miglia crowd, and the Targa Florio was left in Sicily as the last of the great road races.

Sicily was the scene of something else very encouraging, at the end of the 1955 season. C.A.S. (Tony) Brooks, a young English dental student who had never raced abroad, had never even driven a GP car before, came to the Siracusa GP with the latest Connaught and proceeded to outdrive and outpace all the opposition. It hardly mattered that it was the last GP to be won by a car with a preselector gearbox; it mattered rather more that it was the first to be won by a car with disk brakes, though Jaguar had demonstrated their worth at Le Mans in 1953; what mattered most was that it was the first GP to be won by a car of British construction and design – and, apart from its Pirelli tyres, of British manufacture.

C.A.S. Brooks in a Frazer Nash,
a year before he astonished the world

*Centre: Silverstone '55: early
Vanwall nearest, and Connaught, smoothest*

*Below: Aston Martin
handover, Collins to Frère*

Above: Louis Rosier in 1953

Centre:
'55 Vanwalls in the Silverstone paddock

To all the hopeful and faithful, to BRM and Vanwall and Cooper and their supporters, here was a lift to the spirit and a laugh at superstition. Soon, perhaps, they too could start winning. Not always, yet – Fangio had another two World Championships to win before he retired in his 48th year, and then it would be Hawthorn's turn in a Ferrari – but more often.

The tide was slow to turn. Cooper had fielded one of their little streamlined sports cars, with a Bristol engine crammed into the back, in the 1955 British GP; it was slowest of the field, but as the first rear-engined GP car since the days of the Auto-Union it was perhaps a sign that their half-litre racers had proved something. In 1956 the Vanwall showed a surprising turn of speed from time to time but that was all; and the Connaught challenge had faded. Ferrari had taken over the Lancia cars, and the only real opposition came from Maserati.

That winter, Vanwall summoned two consultants. One was a cocky young fellow who, having spent his student days learning to be a structural engineer and second-hand car-dealer, was now making some devastatingly clever little sports cars labelled Lotus: Colin Chapman, if you please, would design a new chassis to justify what was already a very powerful engine. The other man was one of Chapman's mentors, an even better structural engineer but most in demand as an aerodynamicist: Frank Costin was to clothe the Vanwall in the cleanest and most slippery body that the rules would allow.

In 1957, the Vanwall was the fastest car in racing, driven by two of the three fastest men in racing, Moss and Brooks; it was by no means the most reliable in racing, but while it kept going it kept the Italian Establishment gasping. The turning point was reached at the end of practice for the 1957 Italian GP at Monza, when three green Vanwalls stood at the head of the starting order and tears stood in Fangio's eyes as he realised that, for the first time in many years, he could not earn the pole position.

Vanwall did very well indeed in 1958, even though they were down on power. So was

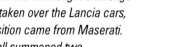

Before the crash: Fitch and Levegh

Before the crash: Fitch and Levegh

Left: Daimler-Benz kept their
GP streamliners for the really fast circuits, as
here on the Monza banking, still in use in 1955

Above: GP Mercedes-Benz, 1955

everybody else: the rules had been changed to stipulate ordinary petrol instead of the alcoholic brews that were the racing engine's staple fare. This was at the insistence of the oil companies, who wanted successes worth advertising. As for the organizers, they wanted occasions worth promoting: that meant shorter races, and more supporting events to fill a programme that might attract the public. As is worked out, the cars carried so much less weight of fuel that they were all actually faster – but they were nevertheless being

Right: Air brake on the Le Mans Mercedes-Benz

Far right: J.M. Hawthorn

Below:
Moss begrimed with brake-dust, and Hawthorn glad of a cleaner cockpit (Mercedes-Benz and Jaguar respectively)

harried, too often for their comfort, by a handful of diminutive Coopers, even less powerful but lighter still and lower and nimbler, respectful neither of tempers nor of traditions…

Change was everywhere. The Mille Miglia had gone, Pirelli had gone, Fangio had gone, the Italian domination of the Targa Florio had gone. Since 1930, the last of the great road races had only fallen three times to a foreign car: a Bristol-engined Frazer Nash in 1951, a Mercedes-Benz in 1955, a Porsche in 1956. From 1958 until it petered out in 1970, the Sicilian epic would be consistently fought

163

Centre, top: GP Connaught, 1956

Centre, bottom: '56 Cooper-Climax

*Below: Haunted by his
record-breaking father: Donald Campbell*

Above: A.C.B. Chapman:
his monogram on every Lotus

Centre: Moss
('56 Maserati) was runner-up in
the drivers' World Championship four times

Above: Dawn mist at Le Mans

Centre: Fangio, Brooks, Moss,
Lewis-Evans – a properly ordered procession

Strip, left to right:

Moss heading for
a Vanwall victory, at Monza in '57

Luigi Musso, '57 Ferrari

Peter Collins, Ferrari

*Right: A German GT race –
mostly Mercedes-Benz and
Porsche, but with a 3-litre Ferrari to add tone*

Below: Mike Hawthorn at the Nurburgring

only by Porsche.

There was the threat – or promise – of greater change to come, from the USA where innumerable hordes had been infected with the fever. Most of

their activities still took their traditional forms, though the hot-rodders were making stupendous progress in straight lines across the Utah salt; but enthusiasm for English and Italian sports cars was boundless. What would come of it? So far, only a handful of blustery Cunninghams at Le Mans, and the Chrysler Hemi engine of shattering power and crippling size, and the sad Scarab GP car. There were some very good American drivers already in Europe, though, and doing well in the best of company. How long, before the New World was once again called in to redress the balance of the Old?

Centre: Eloquent 1958 grid: Vanwall in pole position, then BRM, Cooper, Ferrari

Above, right: Remember Nuvolari

CHANGING ENDS

The take-over by the rear-engined racer was astonishingly sudden; the demoralisation of the saloon-car traditionalists by the new front-drive Mini, laying low the mighty in rallying and racing, was scarcely less so.

More steady and insidious in its development was the growth of commercialism, which made its ends justify all manner of new means. There was a new meanness, of science without remorse, governing the design of cars and of tracks; a new meanness, of economics without independence, governing the ambitions of drivers and the avarice of organizers.

Racing was no longer seen on the roads. Only in principle was it seen in the purpose-built arenas that were now preferred. The same applied to rallying, which had become a formal procession from one timed hammering on an off-highway 'special stage' to the next. In practice, motor sport was seen on television.

Some people took umbrage. More significantly, the cars took wings.

1959 - 1977

REIMS Vᵉᵐᵉˢ 12 HEURES INTERNATIONALES
2ᵉᵐᵉ COUPE INTERNATIONALE DE VITESSE

44ᴱ
GRAND PRIX DE L'A.C.F.
CHAMPIONNAT DU MONDE DES CONDUCTEURS
5 & 6 JUILLET 1958

Full astern, turn about, fast ahead – the rear-engined car was a rarity on any starting grid in 1958, but by 1961 the few remaining front-engined cars in Grand Prix racing were deemed obsolete.

It was Cooper who did it, with a brace of low-powered but light and slender midgets which, with suspension adjustable for geometry as well as for elasticity, cornered faster than cars had ever cornered before. Their first win was with Moss, cunning in a privately-entered car, in Portugal; the factory Cooper, barrelling an oppressively taciturn Australian tactician named Brabham, collected the championships in 1959 and 1960. By the end of the latter year, there was a rear-engined Lotus that was even quicker.

The Cooper was opportune; the Lotus was scientific, not only in structure but also in its novel rear suspension, cornering more swiftly and steadily still. There was something consistently lacking in the quality of its manufacture, however, and the frequency of failures removed it from contention too often for the drivers' peace of mind or health of body. One such accident, early in 1962, ended the racing career of Stirling Moss.

A year earlier he had, in two of the three greatest races of that career (the 1955 Mille Miglia was surely the other), explored the limits of Lotus limpetry in winning at Monaco and at the Nurburgring when hounded by far more powerful Ferrari opposition. There was a new formula for GP racing, limiting engines to 1½ litres (and stipulating the use of self-starters, at last ending the primitive push-start or cranking handle); Ferrari was ready with an effective engine while the resentful rabble of British entrants sought and failed to boycott the new rules. It came so easy to create a competent rear-engined chassis, with such good examples available to copy, and it was a Ferrari which carried off the 1961 championship, driven by the American who had shared the winning Ferrari at Le Mans in 1958, Phil Hill.

Graham Hill, by no means American, won it in 1962 in a BRM; but whoever won it in the years up

Far left, bottom:
Fangio's last race: he finished fourth in the '58 French GP. Here his Maserati leads the Vanwall of Moss and a brace of BRMs

Centre strip, left to right:

Brooks, '58 Vanwall

Moss checks in at a Tour de France control

'58 Monaco: Vanwall leads Ferrari

Above, left: G. Hill, '58 Lotus 16

Above, right: '60 Monaco

Above, left: '59 Goodwood: Aston Martin

Above, right: The TT at Goodwood, '59

Main picture: '59 Aston Martin

*Far right: Aston Martin
at Le Mans, 1959. Roy Salvadori reaches 5,
the winning car, as Stirling Moss leaps aboard 4*

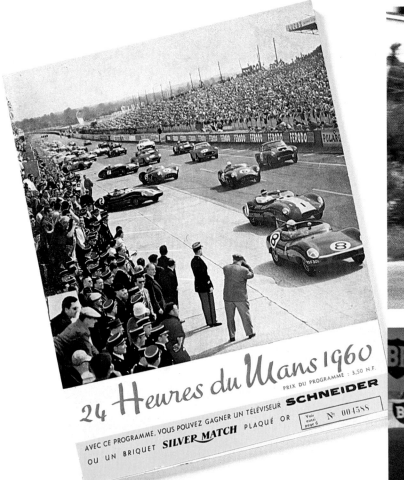

Centre, top to bottom:

Ferraris at Spa, 1961

Ginther, '61 Ferrari

Siracusa '61. Porsche and Lotus 18

Right, top:
The 1961 World Champion, also much given
to winning long-distance sports-car races

Right, bottom: Richard L Petty
prospered as his father Lee did before him,
making the North Carolina family the most
distinguished in NASCAR stock-car racing

Centre, top to bottom:

Cooper

1961 Acropolis rally 700cc BMW

Fording streams used to be a regular
feature of navigational rallies. These ladies
are in the '61 Acropolis event, and are
making the most of Citroën ride-height control

Les Grands Prix de Reims 1962

Ce programme officiel doit être vendu 2 NF.

Volvo, '62 Monte Carlo Rally

Jaguars, '62 Monte Carlo Rally

to 1968, whoever rocketed from oblivion to ovation and back again in those pure and pencil-slim machines, there was no doubt that the most wonderful driver of them all was Jimmy Clark. This shy nail-biting young Scot had a natural ability to drive anything beautifully, tempered by a close working relationship with Chapman so that he will forever be associated with the series of Lotus cars which confirmed that make as the most ingenious, innovative, and effective of a whole generation.

More than any others, it was the Americans who were taken aback by his prowess. When he drove a Lotus at Indianapolis in 1963, they were ready to jeer at the little thing's absurdity; by the time he was cheated into second place at the finish, they were ready to copy the Lotus, just as all the European makers were doing. His car, or his tyres, failed there in 1964; by the time he had the win he deserved, in 1965, he had raised the race average to 150 mph from the 140 at which it stood before his first visit.

Everything was going up, in that decade of fantasy and forthcoming: hemlines rose to uncharted heights, Gagarin went up into orbit, the land speed record went up to 403 mph, and a rear-engined American two-seater coupe went high up the Daytona banking for lap after screaming lap to win the 1965 2000 km race and give Ford the first of the successes they had been trying so desperately to gain with the handsome GT40.

Ford had committed themselves to success in every available branch of motor sport, recognizing in the flowered and free-spending spirit of the decade the truth of the old NASCAR adage, 'the car that wins on Sunday sells on Monday'. Stock-car racing was one of the more obvious of their campaigns, collaboration with Lotus at Indianapolis one of the less obvious; but the most unexpected was their serious effort to win the Monte Carlo Rally – by then, along with Le Mans and the Indy 500, one of the three most influential events of the year.

The 'Monte' was taking evasive new turns. The advantage of big powerful cars in the special stages that were so influential in the results had been reduced by new rules, prompted by the

Far left: Mixed traffic – very mixed –
jams into the first Le Mans corner of 1962

Left, top to bottom:

G. Hill (BRM),
three times victor in the US GP at Watkins Glen

The Summers brothers'
Goldenrod, four Chrysler 'Hemi' engines
made it the world's fastest wheel-driven car

Watkins Glen, NY

Right, top to bottom:

British slingshots
are like toy replicas of American dragsters

Bandini (12 cylinder Ferrari) at Mexico City in '64

Sunbeam Tiger
near the end of the '65 Monte Carlo Rally

French who now only had low-powered cars because of their fiscal system. What they had not allowed for was the incredible versatility of the Mini, the tiny British economy-car which had appeared in 1959. Exploiting its stability and agility with highly-tuned engines and highly-developed driving techniques, countless young people were finding it a vehicle for racing, rallying, or virtually any other sublimation of their thwarted desires; the best of them, selected by a manager of legendary organizational ability, drove the best-prepared examples entered by the factory, and very nearly made the Monte Carlo Rally their monopoly.

The best of them might be as Irish as Paddy Hopkirk, the winner in 1964; but most of them were Scandinavians, because by now most rallies ran their significant stages off the highway, and the snow-bred gravel-bed Finns and Swedes were most practised in the ice-skating and rut-bashing arts. All manufacturers called upon them for aid, not only those like BMC and Citroën who made the most of an engine in the nose driving the front wheels, but also those like Alpine and Porsche who did their utmost with an engine in the extreme tail steering the back wheels. Since all rally drivers made their cars go sideways whenever they thought anybody was looking, such mechanical niceties hardly mattered.

What did matter was that, as pure racing cars grew more and more remote from everyday motoring, as their tyres grew ever wider and more squat (a trend which began in 1965), and as drivers

183

Far left, top: In 1967 there was nothing to compare with a Mini-Cooper S for rallying – even a 1966 model, here driven by Tony Fall

Far left, bottom: Mini, 1966 Acropolis

Main picture: Hopkirk started from Minsk to win the '64 Monte Carlo Rally

Below, centre: Citroën on the Col des Leques, 1966

Below, right: Ford Cortina, '66

shrank low into shrouding cockpits, shirted and shanked in fireproof overalls (not without some unpleasant justification), domed in the full obscurantism of the latest helmets, the public wanted to see some form of motor sport that was more realistic. Conveniently deluded into the belief that the production saloons they saw in rallying bore more than a superficial resemblance to the eponymous contraptions in their local showrooms, they turned their casuist gaze with increasing curiosity on the rallying world; and rallying responded by turning increasingly curious.

In the 1950s (and, in Canada and the USA, even into the 1970s) rallying put plenty of emphasis on navigational skills and timekeeping. As the competition moved off the public highways onto special stages, the co-driver's role became that of calling the corners, from pace-notes prepared during long and intensive reconnaissances. By the 1970s, with Stuart Turner the ace team-manager having left BMC and arrived with Ford, there was very little to prevent cleverly strengthened and raucously powerful small 'production' saloons from being driven through the twitches of an unposted goat-track with as much audacity and commitment as a pure-bred single-seater on a familiar race-track.

There were just a few important rallies where such an approach did not work. One was the annual East African Safari Rally, in effect a fast and hazardous rough-country special stage lasting for four utterly unpredictable days on the edge of the rainy season. Failures were numerous, but in this as in all the longer rallies the major entrants (the car

*Above:
'68 Brabham. Wings are starting to sprout*

Centre: Empathy, Chapman and Clark

Below, right: Watkins Glen '65

Left: Rallying a Rover, Frostick and Boyd

Above: Targa Florio '66

Centre: Porsches in Sicily

Below, right: Ford win Le Mans
at last, and Amon and McLaren win laurels.
A great day for America and New Zealand

Left, top to bottom:

Americans getting the message

Indianapolis '66

Siracusa '66: power returns to Europe

Right, top to bottom:

Architecturally magnificent, the Honda 3-litre V12 was the most powerful engine of 1966. By the time it found chassis and drivers worthy of it, that advantage was gone

Ginther (Cooper-Maserati) in a Monaco hairpin in 1966

Hotel de Paris, Casino Square, Monaco

manufacturers) began to employ a profusion of supporting mechanics, spares, transporters and even helicopters, with quite major rebuilds performed in short order by asbestos-fingered mechanics along the route. Rallying had become just as specialised as racing; indeed it had become a specialised form of racing, with something of the specialities of the Alpine hillclimb and the sporting trial thrown in for good measure.

The usual vicious circle emerged. Because rallying was popular, it was commercially important; because of that, it grew more fiercely competitive; to allow that, the rules encouraged further departures from production-car norms. Sooner or later, somebody would produce a purpose-built rally car.

Lancia did. The Stratos was a cuneiform coupe with racing suspension and a Ferrari Dino engine in the tail – hardly a surprise, since both Lancia and Ferrari were by now satellites of Fiat. After it had won the World Rally Championship a few times, ordinary-looking Fiat saloons were given the job for a few more…

Farce being an always popular form of entertainment, the same kind of misrepresentations was rehearsed in 'touring car' races. The Americans had been putting on the same sort of show for years with their 'stock' sedans; Europe had once been strict about modifications, but that was in the days when racing was done on roads. In the artificial arenas where the crowds were now drawn and the lap-times quartered, road-representative speeds looked pathetic; boredom could only be alleviated by slipping some real racing apparatus inside the silhouette of a production car. Cheats had been getting away with it from time to time since the very beginnings of racing; now it was legal, albeit strictly controlled

Right, top: Brabham, only driver to win a World Championship in a car bearing his own name

Right, bottom: Hulme and Brabham – two World Champions in a two-car team

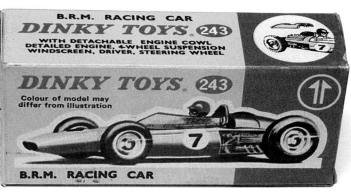

Left: Chaparral cockpit

Right: CanAm trumpets

Seminal, sensational:
the Chaparral, in this case the 2F at Monza

like everything else covered by the bewildering legislation swamping the sport.

At Le Mans, most of the pretence had been discarded: it was a race for 'prototypes', cars which just conceivably could be distantly related to something which might possibly be put into production one day, but which were meanwhile designed for the sole purpose of winning at Le Mans. Porsche (as they did in sports car races everywhere) campaigned like a Chinese army, Ford campaigned like a Presidential candidate, Ferrari complained like a failing husband, all fighting for mastery of the French midsummer. After numerous failures, Ford at last managed it in 1966 and made something of a habit of it for a while thereafter; but in 1967 what made people really sit up and take notice was the debut of a handsome GP Lotus with (to match the new 3-litre formula) a new engine on which the name of Ford was writ large and typically shiny.

It was actually designed and built by Cosworth, but Ford had footed the footling bill and so theirs was the name it bore. It won its first race, and went on to win hundreds in the next 16 years, the quickfire resort of the kit-car kids who could chance up a chassis in a low-rent shop and charm up a fortune from a high-flying sponsor. Comment was kind to them, commerce enriched them, communications blazoned the brans of their breakfasts and the brands of their watches, commonalty applauded the riot of their budgets and the rumps of their women. The stars of the circus were pridefully brilliant, for the god they worshipped was assisting at their rites: television had come to the circuits, and before long it would not matter if the crowds stayed at home.

North American crowds did not stay long to admire the CanAm races, where shovel-bodied two-seaters wriggled and braked and sprinted around tracks curled tight by the blast of bass-throated stock-block American engines. With the broadest tyres and the biggest cylinders of their lusty days, they were all hooves and cucumber; but the first thrill at their romping faded with the realisation that they were all the same, and that the winners were

The East African Safari Rally began
in 1953, and until 1969 was for fairly
standard cars. Conditions are always
tough, and the weather unpredictable:
In 1970 even the winner was 12 hours late!

Overleaf:

Left: Tony Fall's BMC 1800, rallying
from London to Sydney via the Khyber Pass

Inset: Ford Escort performance escalated
rapidly in the late 1960s – too rapidly for some

Right: Tankers and tribesmen obscure
the London-Sydney cars near Peshawur

Pages 196 and 197: The return of power
in 1966 was at first just a matter of making
existing types more robust, to take engines
of 3 litres instead of only 1½. Soon, though,
wings began to sprout…

Previous page:

Left: J. Y. Stewart,
at his best in 1969 with the superb Matra

Right: McLaren, dominating CanAm

Right, top inset: Icon of the '70s:
the CanAm McLaren,
carrying faith and spiritual massage
on a greetings card

Right, bottom inset:
Long-tailed Porsche 907

Opposite page:

Left, top to bottom:

Surtees, '69 BRM V12

Munari, '70 Lancia

Daytona '70: Ferrari and Chevrolet

Centre, top to bottom:

'70 McLaren

Jean-Luc Therier, sliding through
the 1970 Acropolis Rally. The little
rear-engined Alpine kept France
in the forefront of rallying for years on end

Ferrari and Porsche battle at Imola

Right, top to bottom:

Derived from an Indianapolis
Lotus, the beautiful gas-turbine
car for Grands Prix never achieved much

1970 Chaparral groundsucker

BRM patron Louis T Stanley organised a
mobile hospital to attend Grands Prix

Far left, top: By 1970 the traditional Le Mans
start was getting perilous

Far left, bottom: Corvette in its element

Left: Team colour
schemes grew riotous, but some
sort of identification was essential: most
of the TV audience had forgotten how to read

Strip, left to right:

1970 Matra V12

Monza

Rolf Stommelen, Alfa Romeo

1972 Jean-Pierre Beltoise
gives BRM yet another Monaco victory

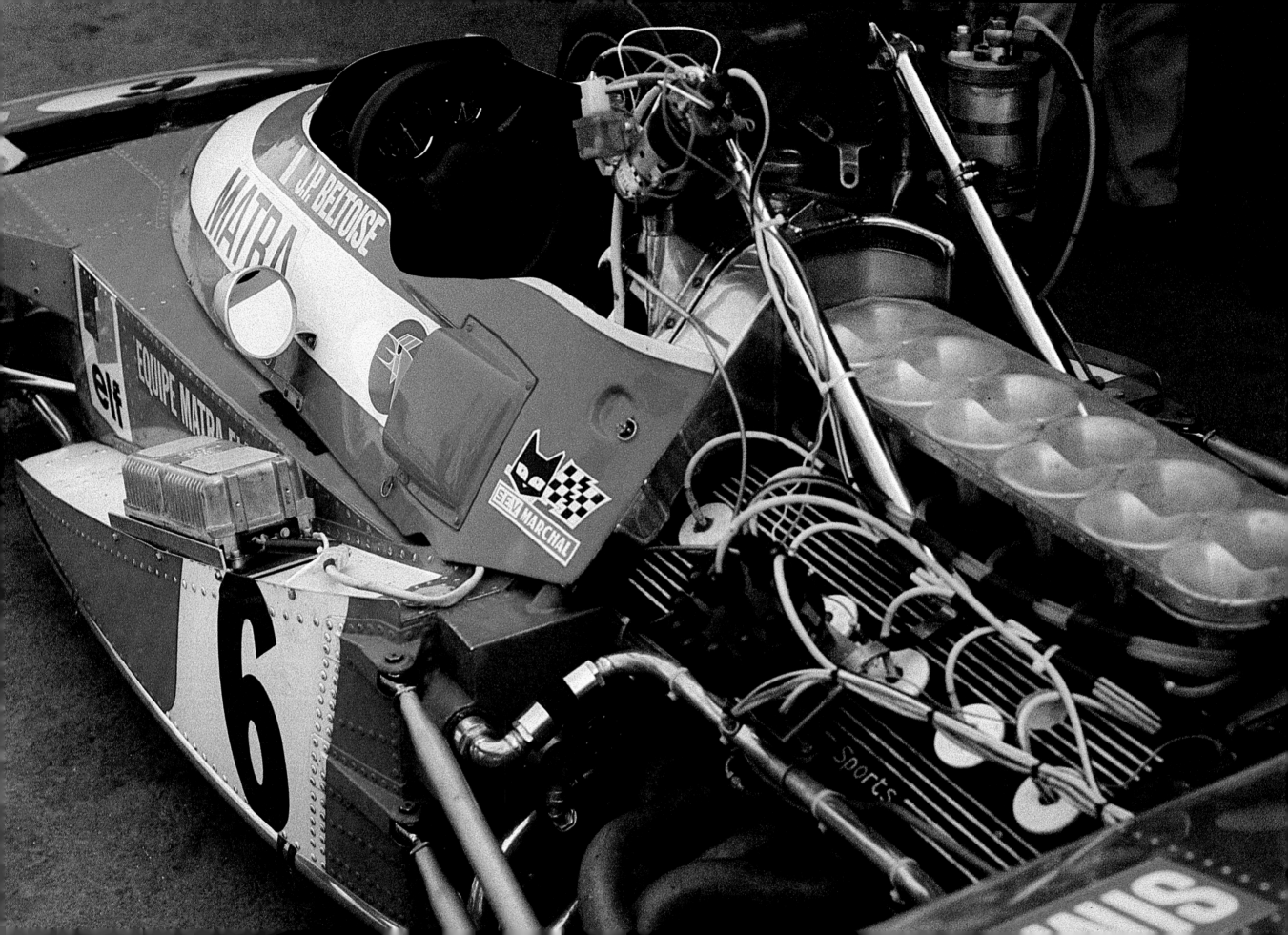

always the same. For years on end, it was
McLaren in a blaze of burnt sienna, until there
came from Germany a flagrantly excessive piece of
engineering with 917 on the chassis-plate and more
than a thousand on the turbocharged horsepower-
chart, and the whole ranting panting CanAm series
disappeared under a Porsche whitewash.

Not that American engines were backward
when it came to a bit of heavy breathing; the drag-
racing fraternity, polishing their craft and scouring
their tarmac at scores of strips across the States,
saw to that. All through the '60s, stock-based
sedans and stick-faced dragsters peeled away the
layers of time and the laws of friction until they had
so foreshortened the standing-start quarter-mile
that it could be covered in less than seven seconds.
Don Prudhomme did it first in 1967, a couple of feet
ahead of a force-fed Chrysler Hemi engine strong
as boilerplate and strident as Babylon.

The Americans had seldom been fooled by the
futile capacity limits to which the European
legislators, as short in foresight as in memory, had
traditionally been addicted. Performance ought to
be measured by absolute terms, not relative ones;
yet, for all the American predilection for muscle,
it was American brain which produced the most
important innovation in all racing. It doubled the
cornering and braking power of the fastest cars,
it realised the potential of the fattest tyres, it
sharpened the aggression of the fiercest drivers,
and it worked on air. It was the wing.

Opel had inverted stub wings on his rocket-on-
wheels in the 1920s, just to make sure it stayed on
its wheels. Michael May tacked a little wing onto
the body of a Porsche Spyder in 1955, hoping to find
more cornering stability. Mercedes-Benz tacked an
airbrake onto their Le Mans cars in the same year,
and found it. In 1966, a little Texan outfit conjuring
CanAm cars in connivance with General Motors did
it properly in the latest Chaparral. That car would
have been rated clever enough if only, as in its very
successful predecessors, for its glassfibre hull, or
for its semi-automatic transmission; but the big
broad wing above its tail, fixed to the wheelhubs
rather than to the body and working together with

Citroën 'raids' for the inimitable 2CV, mostly
across Africa, were the most adventurously
sporting of all. Merely to drive a 2CV is
nowadays thought sporting; but nowadays the
same is probably true of camels

Above, left: Le Mans Matra

Above, right: World Champion sports car of '73 and '74, the V12 Matra

Top, left: Tough, tight and tarmac – the Corsican Rally demanded special preparation, and a different driving style

Top, right: Lancia Stratos en route for Monte Carlo, 1975

Bottom, left: The Fiat Abarth 131 dominated rallying in the late '70s

Bottom, right: Finland's Rally of 1000 Lakes is mostly run on gravel roads

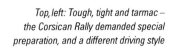

Hannu Mikkola

Lancia Stratos, Acropolis Rally

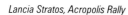

monaco
9-10 mai 1970

24ᵉ
GRAND PRIX
AUTOMOBILE
DE MONACO

PROGRAMME OFFICIEL
PRIX 3 F

British
airways 1000 KMS
WORLD CHAMPIONSHIP SPORTS CAR RACE
Brands Hatch
29 September 1974 12 noon
Organised by the B.R.S.C.C.

INAUGURAL
LONG BEACH

GRAND PRIX
SEPTEMBER 28, 1975

Left: Before the crash:
Lauda (Ferrari) at Nurburgring

Bottom, left:
Sandro Munari in the Monte Carlo Rally

Right: After the crash:
Lauda, miraculously recovered, at Monza in '76

less obvious aerodynamic aids in the nose of the car, worked greater wonders. It forced the tyres down into firmer union with the road, yet brought no significant penalties in weight or drag.

Soon the wing was articulated, and there was no more eerie sensation in racing than seeing the owl-white Chaparral 2F coupé hurtling out of the backdrop woods of Brands Hatch, hushing down on its hunkers into a late-braked corner with the wing at full tilt, the engine then resuming its booming on a steady pitch before the driver feathered the wing and the car rocketed out of the corner on its weird way to victory in the 1967 1000 km race. Never mind the gas turbines, the four-wheel-drivers, the handbrake-turners and all the other cleverclogs of this or any other decade: if the 1954/5 Mercedes-Benz was not the most impressive racing car of all time, then this Chaparral was.

It took the Grand Prix types a couple of years to catch up with the idea, and then they went wild with it. Wings of all shapes and sizes, wings beam-built like bridges, battened like barn-doors, or lashed-up like lattice-laths, were attached in every imaginable place – but sometimes they became detached, and the consequences were frightening. At Monaco, during practice for the 1969 GP, the fright grew so acute that new rules were made and implemented on the spot to limit the size and location of wings. This stopped all the nonsense, but could not stop further exploration of the principle: soon wings were sprouting at Le Mans, where the fastest cars (such as the Porsche which at last managed to win there, in 1970) were exceeding 200 mph along the Mulsanne straight.

If you thought that was fast, you should have seen the cars at Indianapolis in 1977, not merely reaching but actually averaging 200 mph, impelled by a turbocharged version of that eternal Cosworth-Ford V8. And if you thought that was fast, go back to 1970 again, and to the salt flats of Utah, where rocket-propelled tricyclist Gary Gabelich did 622 mph. Call it a milestone if you must, but you would be using the wrong units for the mark he made: for the first time, man had exceeded 1000 kmh on wheels.

Airpipe and helmet
skirt were by '76 part of the
elaborate life-support system for drivers

Lauda

Clay Regazzoni, battle-ready
in a Ferrari

Jochen Mass

The classic 'rail', an American design for
acceleration: lots of power from a highly
supercharged V8 engine, lots of traction, lots
of wheelbase, and very little else but fire and
fury for as few seconds as possible

HIGH PRESSURE

Now the very air was harnessed tightly to the motor-racing Juggernaut. With the advent of the venturi-bellied body, really powerful downforce could be generated aerodynamically in acceptable racers. The simultaneous arrival in GP racing of forced induction by turbocharger made engines far more powerful than ever before.

Both things altered racing completely (the turbocharger, together with four-wheel-drive, would soon do the same for rallying), but the highest pressures of all were commercial. The importance of certain events grew disproportionate, as did the abilities of the extraordinary cars adapted to the likes and loopholes of Le Mans, Daytona, and top-flight rallying where bad accidents brought a sudden change of heart.

Racing experienced a more gradual change of mind, with fuel consumption an added factor. The result is a paradox: the marvels of modern science, heaped on the cars with electronic precision and financial abandon, demand of the drivers more human qualities in mind and body than ever before.

1978 - 1986

*Renault were first with
the turbo charger in Grand Prix racing*

Above: Road markings are bolder now; after all they are approached faster

Previous page:

Left: Le Mans

Right: Brands Hatch

The air, they say, is free; but they, as the history of motor racing so often shows, are not always right. They are only people, after all, like the people who inhabit the motoring world, trapped into thinking only what they are told, coerced into seeing only what they should, pressurised into supporting the causes of commerce, channelled into repetitive grooves under the watchful cursor of the television camera which could never have seen through the dust clouds which raced from city to city, all those generations ago.

The air is very much like people, when deprived of freedom. Imprisoned, coerced, put under pressure and rigidly channelled, air becomes a willing and obedient slave, very forceful and quick to act. By the beginning of 1986, air had supplanted springs in the latest Renault GP engine (with a Lotus chassis around it and Ayrton Senna ahead of it) to unseat each of its valves 5750 times a minute. Air was pushing the representative racing car hard down against the track surface until at top speed the load grinding its sticky tyres into the road was more than twice the weight of the fully laden vehicle.

The air, like people, still manages to break free from time to time. The accident, when the fenced air suddenly shirks its planned path and quits the car's contours to leave it in a tiptoed whirl of unleashed forces, may last for shrieking seconds of ploughed grass and harrowed pride; but sometimes the car catches its wind again, the tyres snatch their grip again, and the instantly disciplined machine shoots straight where – in its driver's flurry of steering corrections – it is pointed.

*Above: F1 flotilla
sets sail in a sea of advertising*

Previous page:
Williams-Honda, by 1985
the most proficient combination of
chassis, engine, and management
systems. Five years earlier, nobody
had even heard of management systems

This page, left to right:

Brabham – BMW

McLaren, with engine by Porsche

A later, lower, Brabham – BMW

Turbo fire

Harry and parry –
close combat in Belgium, 1984

Overleaf:

Main picture: The most overlooked thing
about the forceful Finnish driver Keke Rosberg
is that his name is pronounced Rosebery

Strip, left to right:

Lotus – Renault

Ferrari

Ligier – Renault

Bottom: Williams – Honda

…and soda,
but no ice

The bang into the retaining wall is quick, loud, and perhaps mercifully brief.

The cultivation of safety had been a major preoccupation of racing men in the 1970s. Structures were elaborated, strappings were strengthened, attendants were multiplied and all the trappings glorified to show the paying public what fearful risks their heroes were running for their money. Such was the money to be won, however – and worse still, the money that could be lost – that any device promising better performance would be essayed without hesitation, without concern for any but the intended consequences. The conscience which was roused to quash such ventures was usually that of remorseful rivals outpaced and outsmarted.

Ridicule and the rule-book had been seen in action in an earlier air battle, when Chaparral in 1970 had blown all opposition into the weeds and everything else on the track into the air with a CanAm sucker-car, skirted all around and the air griped from under it by powered fans. Pulled down against the road by the vacuum, the Chaparral hoovered its way around corners faster than anything else ever seen, pursued by clouds of fan-

What men or gods are these?
And whatever happened to heraldry?

Previous page:
Patrese, Benetton Alfa Romeo
and Piquet, Brabham BMW, coming
together dramatically – but with no
personal injury – at the 1985 Monaco Grand Prix

Right: Porsche 917

Marlboro British Grand Prix

Above, BMW pit stop, Tourist Trophy

Opposite: The trouble with racing
wheel to wheel is that when tyres touch,
this can happen – as Derek Daly found out

scoured dust and crowds of angry rival team-managers waving writs of protest. Beaten once again by barrack-room lawyers, Chaparral's back-room iconoclasts withdrew from the arena; but the idea – a perfect antithesis to the Hovercraft which had gone into service in 1966, the year of the Chaparral wing – caught and held like the very tyres it exploited.

It was an English iconoclast who revived it. Chapman shaped the entire underside of his Lotus to create a venturi, and guided the airflow through it from front to rear so that the reduction of air pressure beneath the car would grow more profound as the car went faster. The Italian-born American driver Andretti, his biorhythms conveniently locked into the 1978 Championship calendar, was engaged to augment his vast and varied experience, and the whole of that season was dominated by the combination of Andretti and Lotus – if not by the consternation of other teams.

Aware that they would copy him as quickly as they could, Chapman had a yet more cunning Lotus in readiness. They had him overruled, but in the process the rules were interpreted afresh to render moveable skirts illegal. Nobody was prepared to forego the advantages of an underbody-venturi effect, though, so for a while the cars were practically devoid of springing; and drivers, punished by the bumps, finished blurring races practically devoid of vision. Season by season, sometimes race by race, fresh rounds were fought between convulsive rule-makers and compulsive rule-breakers. Cheats never prosper; if they do, none dare accuse them of having cheated.

227

Rallying still recalls
what road-racing used to be...

...but the road
sometimes takes a bit of finding

Left to right:

Fiat 131 Abarth

Fiat 124

Lancia Stratos

Lancia Rally

Overleaf:

'Where,' as Milton
put it, 'that immortal garland
is to be run for, not without dust and heat.'
(Areopagitica)

Page 233:

Strip, top to bottom:

Lancia Delta S4

Ford RS 200

Lancia Delta S4

Page 234 and 235:

Where, as Bishop Heber put it,
'every prospect pleases, and only man is vile'.

Page 234:

Inset, top: Toyota Celica Turbo 16

Inset, bottom: Co-driver Christian Geistdorfer
and Walter Röhrl with the Lancia Rally

Page 235: Inset, bottom: Bjorn Waldegard
in his Toyota Celica Turbo 16

Page 236: Ex Africa semper aliquid novi

Page 237: Lancia Stratos, Monte Carlo Rally

Some dared to suggest that racing was growing irrelevant to the realities of our motoring life, and that wheeled truth and beauty might be better sought on the snow-flinging and gravel-scrabbling tyres of rally cars. Off the billiard-table surfaces of the racing arenas, nothing so sensitive to ride height as the latest crop of suction-bellied single-seaters could remain controllable; right off the beaten track, where the specialities of the special-stage sprinter came into their own, a different breed of drivers made the demonstration of car-control almost more important than winning. Here too, established ways were about to be overthrown, not by artificially loading all four tyres but by mechanically driving all four tyres. Audi, realising how readily their in-line engines could be connected to the rear wheels as well as to the front, produced the Quattro.

At first it was presented as a roadgoing production car, and everybody was duly impressed. Before long it was tentatively entered in rallies; before much longer, its mildly turbocharged engine had become a raucous raging beast (any engine that big with five cylinders in line cannot help being a bit beastly), and typically specialised hand-built rallying versions propelled by it were running rings around the typically specialised hand-built opposition. Great names were associated with it: Hannu Mikkola, probably the best driver outside GP racing and possibly the best driver alive, sometimes made us wonder whether the virtues he demonstrated were his own rather than those of the Audi – but a man who has been at the top of his professional tree for such a long time cannot be blamed for outshining any new comets lately swum into our ken.

Other drivers confirmed the merits of four-wheel drive. Walter Röhrl, exceptionally fast and safe, became more exceptionally so; Michèle Mouton, elevated to the top rank by her exploits with the Quattro, elevated one up Pike's Peak in record time and gave manly wheel-spinning America a double shock. In record time all the other big firms engaged in rallying were deploying four-wheel-drive variants too.

There was one rather different rally where it had always been a good idea to have plenty of wheels driven, even though the best performances were often made by motorcycles relying on only one. This was the Paris-Dakar rally, as much a test of endurance and intuition as of speed, with the significant portion of it crossing the mountains, the desert, the scrub and some of the forest of west Africa. It was at first no more than an echo of the Baja race which had prospered for years in southern California, a long-distance frolic for dune buggies and pickup trucks; and the Baja event in its turn was a filtered echo of the races which had been run over enormous distances and at insane altitudes in South America. Fangio had cut his racing teeth on them; Daimler-Benz had carved a valuable market with them; but they were remote affairs. The Paris-Dakar rally, by starting in Europe and finishing in Africa, attracted entrants from all over the world and grew commercially important to them all.

Eventually the Dakar too attracted high-powered cars with all the sophistries of turbocharging and four-wheel-drive about them, but they were prevented by the nature of the route from going to such extremes as the cars which confined their rallying to mainland Europe. With so much more traction now available, they could use so much more power, go so much faster, and – as inevitably it would be discovered – have accidents that were so much more frightening. A spate of these, occurring with sudden frequency in the early summer of 1986, prompted a summary dismissal of all the costly cars just built to contest a new and deliberately ferocious category. The drivers and the manufacturers (the latter could still sell cars by rallying lookalikes that were merely twice as strong and fast – there was no need to go to extremes) were probably glad to be relieved of the responsibility.

The track-racing fraternity had the same problem, had been trying for years to find some face-saving way out of the fearful funnel down which they were all so bravely accelerating. Putting limits on tyre sizes had been countervailed by

Previous page: Detroit

Opposite: Turbo heat

This page, overleaf and page 245:

The modern racing car is an assembly of perhaps 20,000 bits and pieces. If assembled 99.9% correctly it will still start from the pits with 20 things wrong

finding aerodynamic ways to load and exploit them, incidentally encouraging the adoption of radial-ply construction in what had been the last bastion of the bias-ply car tyre. Tightening safety regulations had made the cars very much more expensive, and the inflationary cost spiral just made sponsors more insistent on success than ever. For a decade, at least, engine development had come to a standstill, with only the proudest of Italy and France challenging the over-the-counter Cosworth V8 with assorted twelves that were invariably more musical but seldom more mettlesome. In Germany, though, Porsche (who were careful to keep out of direct involvement with GP racing) had put a turbocharged cat amongst the sports-car pigeons; and in France the nationalised and mighty Règie Renault, reluctant to see the decade's richest crop of racing drivers resorting to foreign cars as the challenge of Matra faded, recognised in the turbocharger a new weapon for the fight, and a new justification for involvement.

The turbocharged Renault came into GP racing at about the same time as the venturi-bodied Lotus, but it took longer to be successful. It did not take long to show that a little turbocharged engine could give far more power than an unblown engine twice its size; nor did it take long to prove its reliability, confirmed by a welcome home win at Le Mans in 1978, the Renault's engine being physically the smallest ever to have won the 24-hour race. There were still problems, for drivers and engineers alike, but what motivated all was the need for small engines which could be packed out of the way of the wind tunnels now being contoured beneath every car. Soon Ferrari had jumped on the bandwagon, others went to BMW for help, and the fashion spread like the flames which so often broke from a turbocharger tailpipe.

The first GP win for a turbocharged car fell to Renault, happily in the French Grand Prix, in 1979. The last victory for an unsupercharged 3-litre engine in GP racing was in 1983. By that time, the rules forbidding skirts and false bottoms and all other motoring equivalents of frilly underwear had grown very stringent; but the cursive courses on

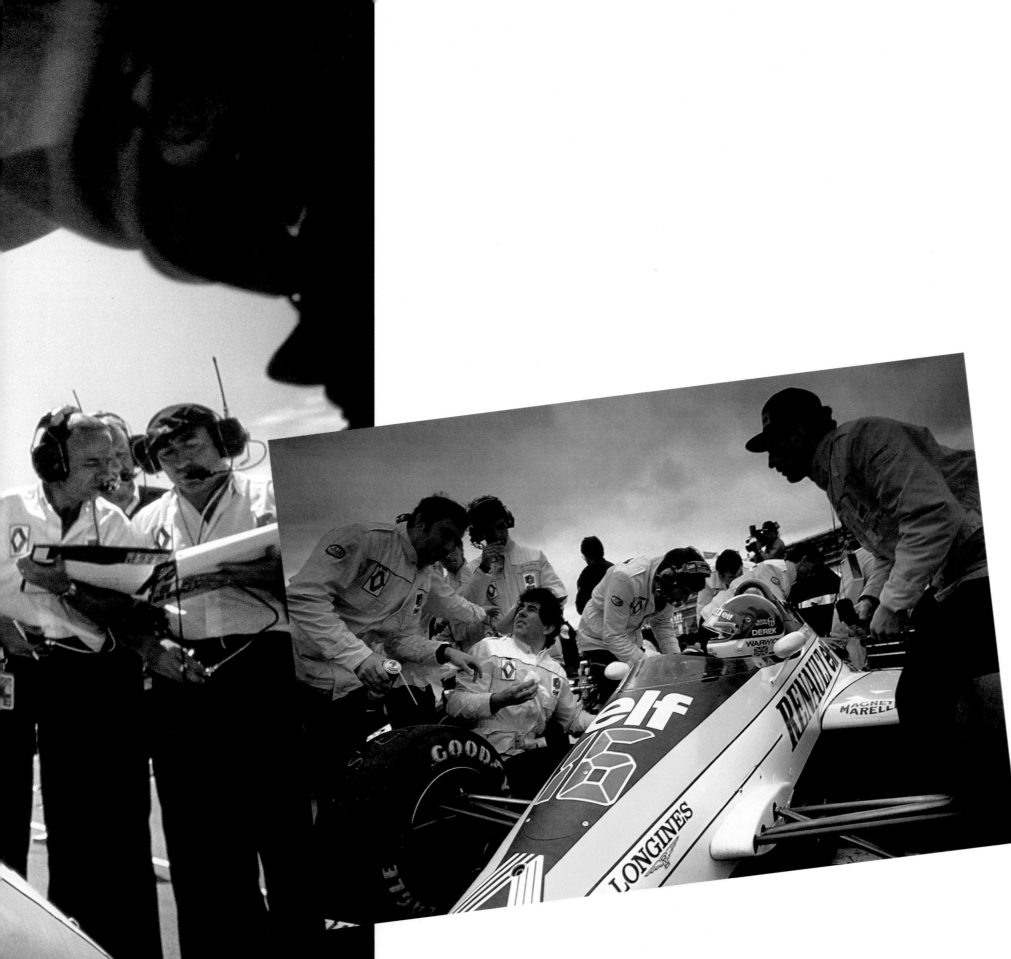

which races were now run gave cornering power the highest priority, and aerodynamic downforce was the only known way to achieve it. Wing effects induced a lot of drag; turbocharged engines could offer enough surplus power to overcome that drag, and still have what it took to make the car go fast.

Very fast. And very loud. And very fleeting in the vision, as brief as the pleasure of the beer in the public enclosures, as transitory as the girls in the paddock, a flash of particoloured advertisements filling the space between four fat little tyres and doubtless enclosing somewhere a driver, a thirsty engine, and a lot of fuel.

Why not limit the fuel? It would be a way to slow things down a bit, to enforce gentler driving. Allow each car just so much, and if it had run out before the end of the race it could not win. The idea had been tried in sports-car racing, where all the technology of Formula One had been amplified by the streamlined bodywork within which a sports car could legitimately be enclosed. It had not prospered, but at least it had served to show the world that sports cars were now as extreme as any and, because their races lasted so long, were even more boring in their irrelevance: Le Mans, for instance, had degenerated into being nothing more than an annual Porsche test-track session. But in Grand Prix racing, the idea of fuel restrictions took hold, and was made to work.

It gave the compulsively clever enormous fun. They knew that the energy in fuel was related to its weight, even though the limit was expressed in volume: anyone who could cram more pounds of fuel into a gallon could go faster or farther. A fine frost formed over the cars on the starting grids, their tanks crammed with fuel chilled to −25°C to increase its density; and a fine froth formed at the mouths of team managers if the start were delayed even half a minute on a hot day, the warmed fuel threatening to burst its bounds as it sought to expand.

Fortunately there were still some vague loopholes in the rules. They stipulated petrol, as they had since 1958; but they had never been too sure just what 'petrol' implied, and now the fuel

Modern racing drivers,
and their womenfolk, are
very serious and cautious people
who do not rush into a situation
without first studying all its implications

companies rose to the challenge, brewing special high-density liquids which packed as much energy into the 195-litre allowance of 1986 as might have occupied 240 litres a few years earlier.

The drivers were still having to take care, short though races might be. The best engines, boosted at four bars, might belt out as much as a thousand bhp. Their supplies would not last long at that rate; a car must cover about five miles per gallon to finish, win or place. But the best engines – and the very best now came from Japan, where the world's best engine-makers were exploiting knowledge gained in the hard-nosed world of motorcycle racing – were now managed by electronic circuitry, monitored by electronic telemetry, and only occasionally undermined by electronic fallibility.

Suddenly the drivers had to be brainy again, as well as brawny. To have neck muscles able to support the head against the brutal heave of cornering forces four times stronger than gravity was not enough; that head had to be shrewd and calculating, able to judge when to turn up the boost for speed and when to modulate it for economy.

Tactics and strategy made lap speeds so variable in the course of a race that the time taken for a change of wheels might no longer be as insuperable a handicap as it had been a few years earlier. Mechanisation and choreography had brought the best pit-crews the ability to fit a complete set of four wheels, their new tyres already heated so as to need no cautious driving until they had reached their proper operating temperatures, in less than eight seconds.

This is the way of sport in the 1980s. Human spirit, the readiness to extend oneself to the utmost, is demanded as relentlessly as when gladiators strove to entertain old Rome; but the amateur spirit, to such extent as it might be at odds with the professional approach, is as dead as old Gibbon. High technology takes much of the credit, and low technology much of the blame, for success or failure with oar or racquet, with boot or ball. Now boots and balls and rowing and racket all have their place in motor sport, yet, simple souls

Left: Ferrari

The Benetton (alias Toleman) BMW became, quite suddenly towards the end of 1986, very fast and competitive

Lotus

Overleaf: The difference between sport and war is that real battles seldom have spectators. The flag-wavers, the cheerleaders, the massed enthusiasts, are buttresses of motor sport, supporting it from outside; the real agonists, the gladiators or drivers, are pillars of the sport, supporting it from inside – and, like Lauda, taking care to fortify themselves, also from the inside

Zella Ziller grüßt Niki Lauda

Success is celebrated in many different ways. It was American drivers who, in the 1960's, first celebrated victory by shaking their champagne and spraying the crowd. The habit has spread.

that we enthusiasts are, we do not fret in our ignorance of who is the world champion rubber compounder or gear profiler, who solders the subtlest microprocessor or marries Kevlar and carbon in the wispiest weave.

But we do know, at the end of each season, who is the world champion driver; and we can see on his breast, at his throat, across his visor, and all around his car, who are the makers of cigarettes and washing machines, of cameras and cooking pots, who pay for him to be promoted and paraded and put at risk of livelihood and life. And that, like the future, may be an easier subject for speculation than the history of all the brain and blood and metal and rubber that have spent a strenuous century getting us here.

Pictures, memorabilia and other illustrative material
supplied by:

Alfa Romeo
Autocar/Quadrant Picture Library
Centro Storico Fiat, Torino
DPPI
Franco Zagari
LAT Photographic Ltd
Phil Sayer
Pirelli
Reinhard Klein
Tamotsu Futamura
The Biscaretti Museum, Torino
The Brooklands Society
The National Motor Museum, Beaulieu
The Tazio Nuvolari Museum, Mantova
Vandystadt/Allsport
(Bernard Asset, Patrick Behar, Arthus Bertrand,
Simon Bruty, Michael King, Jean Marc Loubat)
Vintage

Specially commissioned photography by:

Geoff Dann
Gianfranco Scotti, Eurofotocine, Monza
Richard Mountney
The National Motor Museum, Beaulieu

Martin Lore assisted by:

Gary Black
Jane Charlesworth
Sandra Green
John Szponar
Christine Watkins

Typesetting by Sharp Words Limited

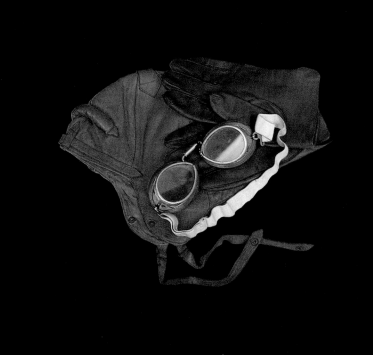